JESUS IN OUR AGE

JESUS IN OUR AGE

A Course for the 13-15 age group

by

JOAN PEDLEY

Head of Religious Education
Blackfen Secondary Girls' School

Illustrated by
Signe Strong

LONDON
BLANDFORD PRESS

First published 1972
© *1972 Blandford Press Ltd.,*
167 High Holborn, London WC1V 6PH

ISBN 0 7137 0571 X

Printed in Great Britain by
Fletcher & Son Ltd, Norwich, and bound by Richard Clay
(The Chaucer Press) Ltd, Bungay, Suffolk

CONTENTS

AUTHOR'S NOTE AND ACKNOWLEDGEMENTS

The purpose of this course is to give young people of 13, 14 and 15 a deeper appraisal of the relevance to life today of the Life and Teaching of Jesus. Discussion is integral to the course and to be encouraged by the teacher. Sometimes it forms part of the introduction to lead up to the assignment.

The assignments proposed can be used by the pupils on their own. The research will give them a basic knowledge of the Life and Teaching of Jesus, while the questions bring out the implications for the present day. At the same time the text was written with the importance of the teacher in mind, whose role has proved salient when the lessons and assignments have been put to the test with pupils.

The assignments were tried out with my own classes; the lively discussions that took place were indicative of the interest aroused. It was found most profitable to go through the introductory passages with them, emphasising points and supplying any further information needed. On occasion the entire lesson has been spent on one point raised, and the remainder left until the next opportunity. Some pupils have found it helpful to discuss certain of the questions before tackling them on their own.

Most valuable has been the teacher's return of the pupils' work, with considered comments, a summary of points made, encouragement to more accurate reading of questions and deeper thought over answers – without any demand that all should think the same.

The first four chapters of Section I were also taken over a period of four months in a mixed class of top academic ability of 13–14 in a Scottish school. The Rev. G. W. J. Mortimer, a specialist teacher of religious education, reported that:

'These chapters provided the class with abundant stimuli for thought and discussion. To probe the possibilities of the text and of the class, I gave unrestricted scope. With intervals of seven days between lessons, there was occasionally need for some recapitulation, but apart from some overlap there was no loss of time. These pupils, at this early stage of their secondary education, found this approach novel at first, and one or two required a little encouragement to overcome initial inertia or puzzlement, but worked well when given a start.'

Where teachers use a thematic approach in the fourth and fifth years, this course has much suitable material to offer. Subjects cover honesty, the family, sex, love, marriage, fear and courage, hate and enmity, differences of race, creed, age and ability and Jesus' teachings as they affect such points, since he tackled at their root these problems and their like in his day.

Scientific investigation entails experiment: so does the search for the truth about God. Information and discussion can prepare the ground, but pupils need to discover and find out for themselves. The more personal questions are given to help pupils to gain insight into themselves and to grasp the ways in which Jesus' teachings might apply to their own lives. Answers to such personal questions need not be handed in – and on this point they must be reassured.

I would like to express my thanks to those who, by their advice and encouragement, helped in the early stages of putting the course into book form; in particular to the Rev. A. G. Loosemore, Adviser in Religious Education for West Riding; the Rev. G. W. J. Mortimer; Miss Mary Fisher, Lecturer in Theology, St Matthias College of Education; the Rev. H. J. Smith, Lecturer in Religious Education, Brentwood College of Education, and Mr Roger Hicks, author of *The Lord's Prayer and Modern Man* and *The Endless Adventure*. I also wish to express my appreciation to Mr Francis Goulding for his help on the text and for the background to the two stories on pages 43 and 94 supplied from his forty years' acquaintance with life in the Middle East; and Miss Vera Frampton of Blandford Press for her personal care at all stages.

J. C. Pedley

PREFACE

This is a series of assignments for you to work out.

The basis of this study is the Life and Teaching of Jesus. The aim is to find what Jesus has to say to us today. This means that there will be some modern affairs and people to read and think about, including our own lives and our own day and age.

The assignments will have an introductory lead which will probably be given by or taken with your teacher. Often this will be short, but sometimes it will consist of a story which forms the basis of your study. At times the research and questions can be done as class or group work, with discussion, but on the whole you will be searching and thinking them out for yourself. At the end of each study your teacher will probably assess your joint findings with you all and this may lead to further questions and discussion. Occasionally a short section specifically for class thought and discussion is given at the end.

To gain the full benefit of these lessons you will need to read carefully all that is written here and be thorough in your research and thinking. Write down your answers clearly so that your teacher understands exactly what you mean. The more personal questions you can think out for yourself, without handing the answers in.

Thought and research are important because no one is interested in uninformed opinion, only in convictions based on knowledge. This knowledge does not only come from books, but also from what we have experienced in our lives. Throughout these lessons you will find many experiments in living which you can try out to gain that experience.

You will need for constant reference *The New English Bible* (N.E.B.), *Revised Standard Version* of the Bible (R.S.V.) and sometimes you may be asked to look up something in other translations such as J. B. Phillips' *New Testament in Modern English* (Geoffrey Bles).

Other reference books are: *God's Hand in History*, Books 1–4, Mary Wilson (Blandford), and *The Living Faith*, Books 1–5, T. G. Platten (University of London Press); also *Stories for the Senior Assembly*, D. M. Prescott (Blandford), *Cruden's Concordance* (Epworth).

Then a shoot shall grow from the stock of Jesse,
and a branch shall spring from his roots.
The spirit of the Lord shall rest upon him,
  a spirit of wisdom and understanding,
  a spirit of counsel and power,
  a spirit of knowledge and the fear of the Lord.
He shall not judge by what he sees
nor decide by what he hears;
  he shall judge the poor with justice
  and defend the humble in the land with equity;
  his mouth shall be a rod to strike down the ruthless,
  and with a word he shall slay the wicked.
Round his waist he shall wear the belt of justice,
  and good faith shall be the girdle round his body.

On that day a scion from the root of Jesse
  shall be set up as a signal to the peoples;
  the nations shall rally to it,
  and its resting-place shall be glorious.

Isaiah 11:1–5, 10 (N.E.B.)

Section I

HUMAN NATURE—AIMS, MOTIVES AND DESTINY

1 What Makes Us Do the Things We Do?

What has Jesus to say to us today? His world was very different from ours. Name some of these differences.

The old saying, 'Reach for the moon', meant wanting the impossible. Today the moon has been reached. In Jesus' day mountains were impassable barriers. Yet Jesus talked about moving mountains (Matt. 21: 21). Today we can fly over and tunnel through mountains, or bulldoze away great hill-sides to build our motorways and railways. These are miracles of science. Is there not an even greater scientific miracle in the creation of the human brain that can conceive and carry out these amazing feats?

But are men and women of today really so different from the men and women of Jesus' day? We have the same kind of bodies and the same human nature. We hate, love, are jealous and generous, feel, suffer and enjoy just like them. Out of these are formed our characters and personalities, as were theirs, to build or destroy, and so this has been ever since man appeared on the earth.

A Ourselves

First we will look at our own human nature.

Questions (written answers which need not be handed in)

1. What makes you want to stay on at school? *or* Why do you want to leave school as soon as you can?
2. Think of the last time you did something for someone without being asked. Why was this?
3. Think of a time recently when you (*a*) did what your parents wanted, (*b*) went against your parents' wishes. Give reasons.
4. When did you last help to raise money for a charity? Say what it was for and why you did it.
5. Such actions show our aims and motives. Put a tick by those you think were good and a cross by those you think were bad.

6. Sometimes we do good things with a bad motive. For instance, in seeing a blind person across the road, what would be a good motive for doing this and what would be a bad one? Sometimes our motives are mixed.

7. Suppose you suddenly realised you were doing a good thing just to show off, would it be right to stop doing it? What would be the right thing to do?

B In Jesus' Day

Research and questions

1. Read Matt. 6 : 1–6. What did Jesus call people who did the right thing for the wrong reason?

2. What was hypocritical about the prayers and almsgiving mentioned in the passage above?

3. What do you think a person means when he says, 'Don't blow your own trumpet'?

4. Copy and underline: *Jesus' teaching was mostly concerned with men's aims and motives, because they are the thoughts that lead to their words and actions.*

5. Jesus often spoke of the thoughts given by God as the good seeds he was sowing. These could develop into useful actions which Jesus called the fruits. We sometimes talk of actions as fruitful. Which parables speak of seeds in this way? *See* Mark 4.

6. A different kind of seed is sometimes sown. Read the parable in Matt. 13 : 24–30. Think of the meaning. Answer these questions with the meaning in mind:

> Who did the enemy represent?
> What kinds of fruit resulted?
> Were they useful or harmful?
> In what way?

7. What is meant by 'Whatever a man sows that will he also reap'? (Gal. 6 : 7.)

In certain countries in Africa still a trumpeter precedes the important chiefs calling out 'Make way, make way for the chief!' Accompanying the chief are also a fan-bearer, an umbrella-bearer and a boy carrying a cushion for the slippers.

2 Finding One's Destiny

Name four people you know of who have, or have had, a ruling aim in their lives.

Say what these aims were.
Life aims can be good or bad. Give an example of each.
Life aims can be too small. Give an example.
What is the greatest aim in life you can think of?

A truly mature and integrated person is one who has found a big enough purpose and whose whole life is geared to it. Most young people do not know what this purpose will be.

Youth is a time for exploring our environment, the world, relationships, of finding our talents and interests. Our aims are apt to change a great deal. We may be quite old before we know our real aim in life and we are never too old to find a bigger one. Some people never do find a consuming purpose and remain immature. Some are satisfied with a small purpose and never fully develop – and the world is the poorer. All the time we are growing our character is forming. It is this which will determine what we do with our talents.

A Growing up

Research and questions

1. What kind of people might the following become, and with what aim in life?

   (*a*) Someone good at mathematics, but dishonest.
   (*b*) A nice-looking girl or boy who has never learned to say 'no' to her/his wrong desires and feelings.
   (*c*) A selfish person with a lovely singing voice.
   (*d*) Someone with powers of leadership, but with hate in his heart.

   Now think and write down what each of these could become if they learnt to conquer their bad characteristics. Would their lives be more useful, or less?

2. Name one person who knew when quite young what his/her work in life was to be.

3. What leads one to think that Jesus was already beginning to be conscious of a special mission in life at the age of twelve? *See* Luke 2 : 42–49.

   All Jewish boys of that age were expected to learn from the Jewish rabbis of the Temple during the Passover festival, but Jesus went further. In what way?

4. When his parents did not understand, did he (*a*) make a scene, (*b*) rebel and refuse to go, (*c*) sulk or (*d*) simply go with them as they wanted?

5. Read Luke 2 : 52. That is all we are told about the way he grew up. He was evidently well liked.

6. What work was he trained to do? *See* Matt. 13 : 55 and Mark 6 : 3. In those days a son usually followed his father's occupation. From all you know of Jesus what would you expect his attitude to his work to have been?

B   Being prepared

Jesus was probably about thirty when he left his home to take up his life's work. Note his patience in waiting to be shown his full destiny.

Research and questions

1. For what immediate purpose did he make this break with his home life? (Mark 1 : 9.)

2. What happens if we rush into a job too soon? How do we feel when we have to wait a long time?

3. Jesus told several parables about the need to be prepared during the time of waiting, e.g. Matt. 25 : 1–13 and Matt. 24 : 45–51. Read these parables and make up a modern parable such as Jesus might have told today. Instead of the master and servant you could write about an employer and a foreman – or a manager and a supervisor – but choose any characters you wish for the story.

FURTHER READING

For those interested in the kind of world into which Jesus was born:
  God's Hand in History Book 2: *The Son of God*, Mary Wilson, pp. 9–10.
  The Living Faith Book 2: *Jesus and His People*, T. G. Platten, Chapter 1.
For more about Jesus' boyhood:
  Jesus and His People, T. G. Platten, Chapter 5.

C Using our talents

Read the Parable of the Talents: Matt. 25 : 14–30.

Questions for discussion

1. In those days a 'talent' was a sum of money, probably worth about £350. Matt. 25 (R.S.V. footnote d).

What does a 'talent' mean today?

Why did the master give his servants different sums of money to look after?

Are we all given the same talents? Do any two of us possess exactly the same talents?

How do we feel about those who have different talents from ours or, as we think, greater ones?

What would the world be like if we were all given the same talents? Would it be as interesting? As satisfactory? In what aspect are all human beings 'equal'?

2. What did the third man waste his time thinking about? What did this make him do with his talent?

What happens to our abilities and talents if we don't use them, e.g. (*a*) our power to walk if we stay in bed for weeks, (*b*) a pianist's power to play at concert pitch if he does not practise, (*c*) an athlete's ability to win races if he does not persist in his training?

When we envy others their talents, what does this cause us to do with our own?

3. In the parable, what was the reward for the faithful servants? How does this shape our ideas about God's rewards – or about Heaven? According to Jesus, what is our life for? For which of the following purposes:

(*a*) to get on in life and achieve our personal ambition?

(*b*) to serve God and do his work in the world – to look after God's property?

What is God's property, according to Jesus?

3 John the Baptist Finds his Destiny

A Spending time alone

We have talked about Jesus growing up. What about his cousin called John? Look up in Luke 1 : 80 (*N.E.B.*) the description of how he grew up. Today for 'strong in spirit' we would probably say 'strong in character' and personality. John spent much of his time in the wild countryside, where he would learn to rough it; to wear clothes that would stand the wear and tear and to eat what he found growing around him when he was too far away from towns and villages to obtain ordinary food.

Research and questions

1. Read Mark 1 : 6 (*N.E.B.*) and write down what John wore and ate.
   NOTE: Locusts are still eaten raw or roasted by Arabs, and honey would be found in the honeycombs of wild bees, tucked away in the clefts of the rocks.
2. Do you ever go off into the country? What clothes do you wear? What sort of things can you find to eat in the countryside?
3. Write down some reasons why in Britain people cannot live out in the open air without shelter for days on end, as it seems to have been possible for John and others to do in Palestine.
4. Do you sometimes go off on your own? What do you think about? What are your reasons for going off on your own? What were John's?
5. Find a poem or piece of prose about wandering in the open air on one's own. Copy a verse or a few lines from this, or make up your own poem.
6. What differences would there be between your countryside and John's? Find a picture of your countryside and one of Palestine (or modern Israel) and stick these in your workbook.

B Preparing the way for the King

In the towns of Judaea, the province where John lived, people were talking of the Messiah* whose coming had been foretold by the prophets. John had listened to such talk for years. Now out in the wilderness he

---

* 'Messiah' is a Hebrew word meaning 'Anointed (by God)'.
'Christ' is the Greek word, with the same meaning.

found himself thinking more and more of this coming, and he began to feel sure it would happen very soon. At some point the thought struck him that he, John, had something he had to do about it; that the people were not ready and he must prepare them. This grew into a very strong conviction. He began talking about it to the people who passed there by the River Jordan. What he said was so new and arresting that the news spread and soon crowds were coming from as far away as Jerusalem to hear him.

Research and questions

1. Write down the words John said about the Messiah's coming as reported in Mark 1 : 7 and 8 (R.*S*.*V*.).
2.   Every valley shall be filled,
        and every mountain and hill shall be brought low,
        and the crooked shall be made straight,
        and the rough ways shall be made smooth;
What do these words make you think of? An order for building a motorway? Bulldozers, tractors and cranes?
Whatever has this to do with the story of Jesus?
To answer this question find first the answers to the following:
   (*a*) Find the passage in Luke 3 (R.*S*.*V*.). Look at verse 4 and find who said these words hundreds of years before.
   (*b*) Whom does Luke describe as fulfilling the role of the 'voice of one crying in the wilderness'?
   (*c*) For whom was the road to be prepared?
3. If you are raising money for a good cause and talk about it to people who are only interested in themselves and hanging on to their money, you cannot reach them unless you can first find a way to break through their selfish aims and so get to their hearts. This was the kind of road that John was to clear, so that people would be ready to appreciate the good news Jesus was bringing.
   People's hearts were blocked with crookedness and mountains of selfishness. Some of the mountains that needed moving were the dishonesty, greed, impurity, hate and pride in which people lived. Can you suggest any others?
4. Find out what the blockages were in (*a*) the general public, (*b*) the tax-collectors and (*c*) the soldiers. Luke 3 : 11–14.
5. What did John ask people to do as a sign that they really meant to change? *See* Mark 1 : 4–5. This was a humiliating thing to ask Jews to do, because so far it had only been asked of foreigners (i.e.

Gentiles whom Jews despised) who wanted to worship the Jewish God. Now John said that everyone needed it, whether Jew or Gentile.

6. Read Luke 7 : 30 and find out which people refused this call to be baptised. Which of the sins (mountains) mentioned at the end of question 3 do you think caused them to refuse?
7. What fruits (Luke 3 : 8) must the people produce to show they were in earnest in undergoing this 'sign' of change? *See* Luke 3 : 11–14.
8. Read part of the Mosaic law in Exodus 22 : 1–6 and write down some of the things expected of the Jews when they had done wrong.
9. Abraham was considered to be the father of the Jewish race, the race of 'God's people'. What did the Jews mean by the excuse in Luke 3 : 8 – 'We have Abraham for our father'? Is it enough to be brought up in a religious home? Does this mean we always live up to our religious beliefs? What more may be needed?

C Removing the blockages

Repentance means more than being sorry. It actually means 'about turn', that is changing one's direction, being sorry enough to give up the old aims and finding new and better ones.

We have been talking of re-moving blockages from a road. We might, instead, talk of cleaning smears off a window. Smears block your vision, so that you cannot see clearly. Wipe off the smears and make the window clean, and you suddenly see the beauty you have been missing.

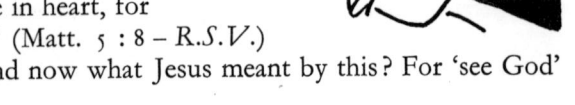

Another word for clean is 'pure': 'Blessed are the pure in heart, for they shall see God.' (Matt. 5 : 8 – R.*S.V.*)

Can you understand now what Jesus meant by this? For 'see God' read 'know God'.

Research and questions (may be taken as a class)

1. Try to explain the saying of Jesus above.
2. Find it in Matt. 5. What do we call the sayings of which it is a part?
3. Name one thing you have been determined to do which has stopped you from seeing that something else was better.

4. Read the following examples of 'Blockages Cleared'. These are both true stories, one very old and one modern.

EXAMPLE 1: ISAIAH (Isaiah 6 : 1–10)

As a young man, Isaiah went one day to the Temple service in Jerusalem. As he watched the smoke rising from the altar sacrifice and curling round the walls catching the light of the flames he felt a great sense of wonder and beauty. It seemed to him that God was there, up high among the clouds of smoke. Some of the smoke curls appeared as angels' wings. As the music rolled around him he seemed to hear the angels singing, 'Holy, holy, holy is the Lord of hosts: the whole earth is full of his glory.'

Isaiah was face to face with the greatness, power and wonder of God. In contrast he felt small and full of evil, and he saw the evil in his nation.

He cried out, 'Woe is me, for I am lost; for I am a man of unclean lips, and I dwell in the midst of a people of unclean lips; for mine eyes have seen the King, the Lord of Hosts.'

In his vision he saw an angel take a live coal from the altar and touch his lips, burning away the evil within him and leaving him fresh and clean – a new man. Now he could hear the voice of God asking, 'Whom shall I send to change the evil hearts of my people?' Perhaps God had been asking that question for a long time, but he had not heard it before. He answered at once, 'Here am I! Send me.'

From then on, his purpose in life was to take God's message to his nation. He was perhaps its greatest prophet. Kings sought his advice, especially at times of danger.

For discussion

Was Isaiah's experience just imagination? Are you different after you have imagined something? Was Isaiah different afterwards? If you are different afterwards you have had a real spiritual experience.

Making a friend out of an enemy

EXAMPLE 2: MAGDI

In Eritrea, Africa, an eighteen-year-old student named Magdi, who attended the Camboni school there, became thoroughly sick of all that was wrong in the world around him and in his own country. He planned to leave school and leave Africa, and to settle down in Canada away from it all.

One day in school he was asked to summarise a book. He went to the school library and found one called *Remaking Men.** He chose it because it was the smallest book there and would involve less work – or so he thought! It fascinated him. He made his summary, but he also began to put what he read into practice. He was honest with his father, asked his sister's pardon for treating her as an inferior, and his teacher's pardon for cheating in examinations. These actions surprised and affected the other students and some of them began to follow his lead. Soon there was a new unity in the school, brought about by the honesty of a number of students.

Magdi realised this was the way to build unity in the world. There was hope after all. He gave up his idea of escaping to Canada, and decided to stay in Eritrea and build with others the same unity in his country as he had begun to build in his school.

Through getting rid of the blockages in his own life he had found new hope and a new adventurous aim in life.

Questions

1. What were the blockages in Magdi's life?
2. What was the new outlook he found when he was rid of these blockages?
3. Is it open to everybody to act as Magdi did? If so, how should one start?

* By Paul Campbell and Peter Howard (Blandford).

4 John the Baptist's Qualities

A prophet voice

We have heard how John lived out in the country by the River Jordan, feeding on what he found there and dressed in a strong camel hair cloak, tied round the waist with a strip of leather. He seemed very much like one of the stern prophets of old, and people flocked to hear him because that is what they thought him to be.

A prophet is one who has a message from God to pass on to the people. For several hundreds of years there had been no true prophets. The Jews had been living, not by the word of God in their hearts, but by their laws and traditions, rites and ceremonies. Some of these were the laws of God, given to Moses and others to help them to live happily and successfully as a community, but the Pharisees had made so many additions that it was impossible to remember them all. These additions were often petty rules to do with outward observances, like washing themselves and their crockery before meals in case they had been in contact with any Gentiles who were considered to be 'unclean', or not walking a step over a mile on the Sabbath. The day of rest had become a day of hard-and-fast rules, regardless of needs. For instance, Jesus was told he should not work on the Sabbath even when he was making someone well. These were certainly not like the helpful rules God had given to Moses, and which are still needed today for the health of community life.

The prophets had always stressed that God is concerned not with outward observance but with the thoughts and aims in men's hearts (Micah 6 : 7–8; Isaiah 29 : 13). But now it was as though true religion was dead and men were no longer directed by the living God but by the orders of the scribes and Pharisees.

John the Baptist, though his story is told in the New Testament, was in the true line of the great prophets of the Old Testament, bringing God's live directions back to the people. A change was needed before the Messiah came. The Jews needed repentance and baptism. John's work was to pass on this message – the call to repent and start living God's way. Many people accepted this call but, as we have seen, most of the scribes and Pharisees were too proud.

Research and questions

1. The scribes had evidently been saying that before the Messiah came the Jews would be visited by one of the old prophets. Find out which prophet this was. Mark 9 : 11–13.

   John certainly seems to have modelled himself on this prophet. In what way did he live like him? *See* 1 Kings 17 : 1–6; 2 Kings 1 : 8.
2. Give an example of an outward observance today which is meaningless unless it is done with the whole heart.
3. Write down two of the laws of Moses which are still necessary today. *See* Exodus 20 : 1–17.
4. Find out what Jesus said we needed to do before our worship of God is real and not just a matter of form. Matt. 5 : 23–24.

B Unshaken

In Mark 9 : 11–13 Jesus said that Elijah (John the Baptist) had returned already and men had done to him 'whatever they pleased, as it is written of him'.

Research and questions (*may be taken as a class*)

1. What had they done to John the Baptist? If you have forgotten, read Mark 6 : 14–29.
2. Find out from this passage *why* this had been done and explain John's great courage.
3. What did Jesus think of John the Baptist? Luke 7 : 24–30.

4. What do you think Jesus meant by 'a reed shaken by the wind'?
If possible, listen to the record, 'Are you a man who goes where the
wind blows?'*

For discussion

Who really affects the age in which he lives, the man who stands firm
on what is right, or the man who changes his opinion as the fashion
changes? *For private thought:* Which of these am I?

C Living to make another person great

St John's gospel makes a further point about John the Baptist. He was
prominent until his cousin, Jesus, came on the scene. He then drew
attention to Jesus' greatness and was content to let him attract the
crowds (John 1 : 26–30; 3 : 25–30) while continuing with his own
work. Later (John 4 : 1), Jesus heard it was being said that he made
more disciples than John. What did Jesus do? John 4 : 3.

Research and questions

1. Do you think it was easy for John to accept Jesus' greater popularity? Do we normally find it easy to take a back seat and help to
make our brothers, sisters and cousins great, forgetting ourselves?
2. Which of the following adjectives describe John the Baptist – timid,
brave, selfless, swayed by other people's opinions, committed to
God?
3. Write an essay: 'An Appreciation of John the Baptist.'

* From gramophone record 'Il est permis de se pencher au dehors' or 'Anything
to Declare' (*European Musical Revue*).

5 Jesus Enters His Vocation

A Called by God: Jesus' baptism

Jesus' baptism was a great spiritual experience. How do you think his disciples knew about it? Read how it is expressed in Matt. 3 : 13–17, Mark 1 : 9–10 or Luke 3 : 21 and 22.

John the Baptist thought of baptism as repentance for sin. Matthew tells us that John felt it was he who should have been baptised by Jesus, not the other way round. But Jesus felt God wanted him to be baptised and was willing to identify himself with sinful man to obey God.

During this baptism God showed that he had set Jesus apart for a different life. As Jesus was baptised, he accepted all that it meant to be the one and only Son of God. And quietly, like the flight of a dove, came God's Holy Spirit of Power to help carry it through.

Research and questions

1. Think of an experience which has meant a lot to you, something about which you *felt* a great deal. Perhaps it was the first time you saw a breathtaking sight, e.g. mountains in Switzerland. It may have been a sad experience in your life, or an exciting or startling one.

   Try to express this inward experience in a few sentences.

2. John Wesley, first of the Methodists, found his vocation in life after a spiritual experience. Find out about this.

3. Paul's life work began with such an experience (Acts 9). Explain shortly.

4. Name others with such an experience to set them on their life's work.

5. How was the experience described in *one* of these cases, or in the case of another great man or woman?

SOME EXAMPLES IN THIS CENTURY:

David Wilkerson: *The Sword and the Switchblade* (Hodder & Stoughton), Chapter 1.

Dr Frank Buchman as described in *Frank Buchman's Secret* by Peter Howard (Heinemann), pp. 18–21.

Brother Andrew: *God's Smuggler* (Hodder & Stoughton), Chapter 4.

6 Conflict and Certainty—Jesus' Temptations

After the public act of Jesus' baptism, the question was how to work out the call to bring people back to God. This needed much thought, to consider every method possible, to reject wrong and choose right courses. For this purpose Jesus felt himself driven into the wilderness – that same deserted tract of Judaea where John had lived so long. He was there for forty days.

He thought of a number of ways of winning people, ways which looked good at first but on further reflection were seen not to be the right ones and so were rejected. As there was no one with him, anything we know of that time must be what Jesus himself later related: he told of three particular choices which faced him there. He described them as a conflict between Satan and God, between evil and good, as the controlling force to guide his actions. He called them temptations. It is important to remember that temptation is not the same as sin. When we are tempted, we are conscious of a pull towards doing something that seems attractive. If we decide it is wrong and still do it, that is sin.

Food that satisfies – Jesus' first temptation

He naturally grew hungry. In front of him were stones shaped like loaves. The thought struck him – why not use your God-given power to turn these stones into bread? Perhaps he had the further thought that the many hungry needy folk in his nation would be impressed by the power to provide food and meet material needs by changing stones to bread. But he knew that what he was looking for was much more than bread or the staying of a momentary need that would recur. He was looking for God's guidance on his whole path in life. Nothing less would satisfy the need inside him. Nothing less would satisfy the need inside his people. He saw the idea as a temptation of Satan and rejected it by recalling the words Moses had said, according to Deut. 8 : 3 : 'Man cannot live by bread alone but by every word God utters.'

Research and questions

1. Read how this first temptation is described in Matt. 4 : 1–4 (N.E.B.). Copy out the words of Jesus' reply, 'Man cannot . . . God utters.'
2. Older people are always telling young ones how much better off they are than the older generation was at their age. Name some of the things most people have today which were once only for the rich.

3. Are people happier now? Have they stopped wanting more?
4. Name some societies which give material aid to the hungry and underdeveloped parts of the world. Did Jesus' answer mean that those who followed Christ should stop doing this work? If not, what did it mean? To help you to answer this question read Mark 6: 30–44. Jesus gave them food. What else did he give the people that day?
5. Jesus' answer and his life on earth showed that all who follow him should live (*a*) for others, instead of living only for themselves and their families, and (*b*) to satisfy all the needs of others; the needs of their bodies for bread, the needs of their minds and hearts for spiritual direction from God.

   (i) Discuss the statement and see if you agree.
  (ii) Which parts of the world are especially needing food for their minds? Find out what some societies are doing about it.
 (iii) How do we find spiritual direction from God?

B Prove it! — Jesus' second temptation

Matt. 4 : 5–7

Jesus knew how men demand proof. He was very tempted to give them what they would want. He appeared to be standing on the parapet at the top of the Temple where all the crowds were gathered below. The voice of the devil whispered that if he threw himself down before them and landed safely, they would believe that he had been saved by God. The Scripture said: 'He will put his angels in charge of you, and they will support you in their arms, for fear you should strike your foot against a stone' (Psalms 91 : 11–12). The people would remember this prophecy and believe that he was the promised Messiah.

But would anyone change? Would it do any good? People would crowd to hear him wherever he went just to see him perform some other spectacular sign, but nothing would be different. He would only be a passing wonder.

It was not right to listen to men's demands for proof. His job was not to put God to the test, but to do God's will in the world. This was only another temptation of the devil. He remembered a further quotation from the Scripture and said firmly, 'You shall not put the Lord your God to the test.' (Deut. 6 : 16 – R.*S.V.*)

Research and questions

1. Look up some occasions when men demanded proof of who Jesus was: Mark 8 : 11–13 and Mark 15 : 29–32.
2. Which people demanded the sign in each case?
3. In what way was the sign demanded in Mark 15 rather like the one in the second temptation?
4. In the years which followed this time of testing in the wilderness Jesus was to give the people plenty of signs, as God directed him, but not when people demanded them. 'If you have ears to hear, then hear', said Jesus at one point (Mark 4 : 9). He quoted the Jewish Scriptures in Mark 4: 12. What was it that people were not willing to do which made them appear to be blind and deaf to these signs?

5. *For private thought*: When someone suggests you need to change, what do you do? Do you turn a deaf ear, or listen carefully and consider if there is some truth in it?

Make people obey – Jesus' third temptation
Matt. 4 : 8–11

From the top of a hill people and buildings below look like little toys and we can see a long way. We have a feeling of power. Have you ever felt like this? Such an experience symbolised Jesus' third spiritual battle in the wilderness. Was he to become, as the Jews expected of the Messiah, a king greater than David, subduing his enemies and forcing people to obey the Law as the Jews understood it? He would have at his side all the patriotic Jews longing to overthrow Rome.

But this was not what he had come to do: 'My kingdom does not belong to this world. If it did my followers would be fighting . . .' (John 18 : 36), he said later. He was not to win outward allegiance as an earthly king, but inward allegiance of the heart. You cannot win love by force. To choose what the Jews expected would have meant compromise. It would have meant working with the wrong means and it would have achieved the wrong end. For this reason it was not God's perfect way but the devil's (Satan's). He had to choose which of them to serve. He gave his firm answer, 'Begone, Satan! For it is written, "You shall worship the Lord your God, and him only shall you serve." ' (Matt. 4 : 10 – R.S.V.)

Jesus had now faced three ways of working. He saw them all as temptations to bring about God's kingdom in the 'world's' ways, as short cuts prompted by the devil which would, in fact, have prevented him from accomplishing God's purpose. Rejecting them, he saw his way clear. Matt. 4 : 11 (R.S.V.) says, 'Angels came and ministered to him.'

Which way did Jesus take? Did he already know that it would lead to the cross? See what you think as you go on studying this course.

Research and questions

1. Find two occasions when the Jews, thinking of Jesus as the Messiah, tried to make him become their earthly ruler: (*a*) John 6 : 15. What event had just taken place which the people took as a sign that he was the expected Messiah? (*b*) Matt. 21 : 1–11, 14–17. In this event, how did Jesus show that he was not to be a conquering king in the way people expected, but that he came in peace, king of all those who were humble enough to choose God's way in their hearts?
2. There is a sense in which Jesus, the man, in all his temptations, was the observer of a battle going on between two Powers. What would you call these Powers? Do they battle for the service of every human being?
3. Read again the last part of the introduction to this section on page 27. Note what is said there about temptation and sin. Then try to explain in your own words the phrase: 'You cannot help crows flying over your head, but you can stop them nesting in your hair.'

4. Jesus' temptations were all to do his work in the wrong way. Are you ever tempted similarly? What are some of the wrong ways to do these assignments for instance – or your Saturday job, if you have one? What is the right way? Is it true that if we have the right motives we are more likely to hit the target? Explain.

Section II

PEOPLE CAN CHANGE— THE SPIRIT THAT CURES

1 The Spirit of Victory

In this section we shall study the way Jesus worked and what it can mean for us today.

Jesus began his work in Galilee. According to the Synoptic gospels (Matthew, Mark and Luke), he spent most of the next (probably) three years teaching and healing there, ending with his final visit to Jerusalem to the Passover and his death and resurrection. John's gospel makes it appear that he went to Jerusalem at other times. Perhaps he did attend other Passover festivals; we do not know. John was more interested in drawing out the spiritual truth of what had happened than in keeping to a chronological order.

Jesus built a team to work with him and to carry on after he had died. We shall not be concerned with the disciples until a later section of this book, but they were always present.

A Victory over wrong

What are some of the things that are wrong in the world and need changing? Do you believe they can change? Do you think you can do anything about them? Suppose someone came along and proved that from now on these things *could* change. Would it be good news?

What do you think God's kingdom is? Jesus said it 'is at hand'. It came to men with his coming. We can experience it now, when we accept God's rule over our lives. Our defeatist attitude can change, and things around us will change too, as we do.

Jesus did not only *say* this. He began to prove it by demonstration. One of the great problems of his day was the number of apparently incurably ill and unhappy people who had given up hope. He showed them that they need not be defeated by these things; he healed madmen, lepers, the paralysed, and men and women with many other sicknesses. This was one way of demonstrating that God's rule meant victory.

Research and questions

1. Which word in Mark 1 : 15 means 'good news'?

2. Make a list of six people whom Jesus healed. Use your Bibles and write down the references.
3. Did Jesus heal everyone who was ill? If you find occasions when he did not, look for and give possible reasons.
4. Did Jesus just pick people to heal at random? What happened first? Mark 5 : 23, Luke 7 : 3 and 9 : 38.
5. What did he ask of people before he healed them? Mark 2 : 5 and Mark 5 : 34, 36.
6. Why did he not heal many people in his home town, in and around Nazareth? Matt. 13 : 58.

Further work

Find out more about the problems of Jesus' day and make a list of similarities with the problems in the world today.

FURTHER READING

The Living Faith, Book 5: The Word and the World, T. G. Platten, pp. 19–21, 'Preaching and Healing'. This is a good chapter on Jesus' healing, particularly his healing of people with mental disorders, who were then thought to be possessed with demons. See also pp. 34–35 'The Madman of Gadara'.

B Victory over a physical handicap

Here is the story of a boy who refused to be defeated by a physical handicap. His name was Peter Howard. He was born with his left ankle joined to his knee, his whole calf bent in a semicircle. His leg was cut and straightened, but the doctors held out little hope of a permanent cure. In spite of many visits to the doctor and much manipulation and massage, as he grew older his foot turned inwards and his leg remained twisted and thin. For years he wore an iron on his leg. Yet neither his father nor his nurse took any notice of his lameness – and nor did he. In early years the only difference between his life and that of his fellow schoolboys was that he had to go to bed ten minutes earlier to be massaged.

A boy who was later at school with Peter reported that the sock on Peter's thin leg was always falling down. When he was tired his leg dragged, but he was always dashing about and getting hot and dirty. One of his nicknames was 'Beetroot'. Like most boys he was ready for a fight at any time and was sure to be found in the thick of it. He loved football. One day on the rugger field he fell and sprained his ankle. The doctor who examined the sprain told him 'Cricket is a better game

for you. Don't play football. You stick to cricket, there's a good boy.'

At that moment Peter began to want more than anything to become a footballer. He took no notice of the doctor's advice. A very persuasive young man, when he went to Mill Hill school at the age of thirteen, he sought out the school doctor and got him to agree that if his parents allowed it he could shed his leg-iron and play games. He was soon playing hard and developed a rollicking gallop in place of the fast running of the other boys.

Some years later he acquired a motor-cycle. One day he was riding home for the holidays when he collided with a truck and found himself in a ditch, bruised and bleeding. Assuring the truck driver that nothing was wrong, he borrowed a pedal cycle and cycled twelve miles to the nearest hospital. There it was found that his lame leg was broken in two places. Awaking from the anaesthetic he overheard the doctor saying, 'I shall have to take his leg off'. That was a terrible shock. He begged for his parents to be consulted first. In the end he was able to keep his leg but had to spend four months in hospital.

When he returned to school he went straight into the Second XV Rugby team. Later he was in the First XV and opening bat for the First Cricket XI, as well as being a member of the Boxing Eight. At the end of his school career he was proclaimed senior champion in athletics. He had a tremendous capacity for enjoying life. His Rugby playing continued at Oxford where he gained his Rugger Blue. Then in 1930 over the radio he heard his name announced as one of the players picked to represent England. He played for England a number of times and became captain. This was the height of his sporting career.

What Peter Howard learned about being victorious over his physical handicap he carried into all he did in life after University days. He became a Fleet Street journalist and married a Greek tennis star, Doris Metaxa. Some years later he met a force of people out to put right what was wrong in the world under the guidance of God. Now Peter saw his true purpose in life and all that his earlier training had fitted him to do. He put into it all the determination and belief in triumph which he had put into rising above his physical handicap. He became the world leader of Moral Re-Armament, travelling all over the world, speaking, meeting people, writing plays performed in London and many countries abroad. Among his audiences were many students. He was not living now for his own fame but caring for hundreds of individual people and seeking God's mind on how to help them to rise to their destinies. Death came to him at the height of his work, when he was doing battle in Peru for the South American people to find God's plan. Behind him he left hundreds whom he had inspired to carry on this fight across the world.

(Based on *Peter Howard: Life and Letters* by Anne Wolrige-Gordon.)

Research and questions (Answers to 1–3 need not be handed in)

1. What do you do when you are ill or hurt? Do you enjoy being fussed and wallow in being ill? Are you full of self-pity? Or are you determined to get well quickly?
2. Is there anything else in your life about which you sit down and moan instead of rising up and tackling it?
3. Do you run away from difficulties, or do you face them? Why?
4. Find out and write briefly about one other person who has risen amazingly above a physical handicap.
5. Copy out Mark 11 : 22–24.

SOME SUGGESTED BOOKS

I Walk on Wheels, Elisabeth Sheppard-Jones (Bles).
The Story of My Life, Helen Keller (Hodder & Stoughton).
Reach for the Sky, Douglas Bader (Collins).
God's Second Door, J. H. Roesler (Association of Mouth and Foot Painting Artists).

C   Victory over temperamental handicaps

The title to this section is 'The Spirit of Victory'. It is the spirit within us which makes us what we are. There are those with a happy spirit, a jealous spirit, a greedy spirit. Think of other adjectives that describe the different kinds of temperament.

John the Baptist said that when Jesus came he would 'baptise you with the Holy Spirit', i.e. people would receive the Spirit of God. We

have seen Jesus bringing cure to those who previously appeared incurable. The Spirit of God, the Holy Spirit, is a Spirit of Victory.

Jesus sometimes had to change a person's spirit before he could heal him.

Research and questions

1. Remind yourself of the healing of the paralytic in Mark 2 : 1–12. Do you know anyone who is paralysed or partially so? It takes tremendous will and courage in such circumstances to make the effort to become mobile.

2. The men who brought this man to Jesus had faith. How did they show it?

3. The paralysed man had, apparently, an idea which gave him a defeatist spirit. Like others in his day, he felt he was ill because he was a sinner and so did not deserve to get well.

   What did Jesus say to change him?

4. Jesus might have said, 'Don't be silly! You are no more a sinner than those who are well', or 'You are not a sinner. Snap out of it!'

   How much do you think that would have helped?

   If you *knew* you had done some things wrong, would you feel any different if someone said those things to you?

5. 'Forgiven' has the meaning 'wiped out'. Why do you think 'My son, your sins are forgiven' was more helpful to the paralysed man? How would it change the man's spirit and help him to be healed?

2   The Spirit of Truth

You could think of the troubles in the world as a kind of disease. Jesus did. Look up Mark 2 : 17. To cure disease an operation is often needed. What does the doctor have to do first? He has to find out the cause. For that he needs an X-ray or some other form of strong light.

Jesus said, 'I am the light of the world'.

Where do you think the troubles of the world really lie? Some people think they lie in the system of government – in the economic system – in the political party they do not agree with. Discuss what *you* think. Jesus thought they were in people. He did not start by trying to change the system. He began to change people. First he shone his light, clearly showing up what was underneath. He had a wonderful understanding of what people were thinking and were like inside.

A   Truth tackles smugness and hypocrisy

Research and questions

1. Which of the following parents give the best kind of love to their children:

   (*a*) those who persuade themselves that their children are wonderful and can do no wrong;

   (*b*) those who 'give in' to them even when they feel it is unwise;

   (*c*) those who say 'No' to what they regard as wrong;

   (*d*) those who understand what their children feel but expect and help them to make the right decisions?

   Explain why you give your answers.

'Our child is wonderful'

2. Look up the reference in the Bible to Jesus' saying, 'I am the light of the world.' Use a *Concordance* to find it.
3. Notice how often Jesus read people's thoughts. Whose thoughts did he read in each of the following cases:

> Matt. 12 : 25
> Luke 6 : 8
> Luke 9 : 47
> Luke 11 : 17?

4. If you are a person who likes to look good on the outside, but gets away with all kinds of wrongdoings on the quiet, do you think you would have found Jesus a very comfortable person to meet face to face? If not, why not?
5. Read Mark 7 : 6–13. Here Jesus is tackling people like the one in question 4.

(*a*) What was the teaching of God about one's parents in this reading?

(*b*) What was the tradition the elders had made? 'Corban' meant a money gift set aside for God. Once set aside the Pharisees said it could not be used for any other purpose.

(*c*) How were the Pharisees who kept this tradition in this case breaking God's law? Do you think they would have been using the money for God if they had given it to their parents when they were in need? Explain.

(*d*) What did these men care for in their hearts more than their parents or God? Jesus made them face themselves honestly.

For discussion

1. 'You will know them by their fruits.' (Matt. 7 : 15–20 – R.S.V.)
2. '. . . whatever goes into a man from outside cannot defile him. . . . What comes out of a man is what defiles a man.' (Mark 7 : 18–23 – R.S.V.)
3. '. . . where your treasure is, there will your heart be also.' (Matt. 6 : 21 – R.S.V.)

B Truth tackles dishonesty

Jesus was tough with smug people who would not face their need for change. But with others it was his caring which brought honesty on their part.

Read how Jesus treated Zacchaeus. Luke 19 : 1–10.

Research and questions

1. How did the people and their leaders treat tax-collectors, and why? Notice what they murmured (Luke 19 : 7). Do you think Zacchaeus was a lonely man? For what reasons?
2. Notice that he *wanted* to see Jesus. Do you think he would have wanted to if he really wished to continue his deceitful life? If not, why do you think he had not given it up already?
3. What did Zacchaeus do to show he was in earnest about changing his heart and his ways? Why is such action important for wrong done?
4. Are there some people whom you treat as people treated Zacchaeus? Does it make them any better?
5. Find out what Jesus said we need to do if we want others to change: Matt. 7 : 4–5.

Suggested activity

Arrange a very short play-reading from Dorothy Sayers' *The Man Born to be King*: the fourth play, *Heirs to the Kingdom*, p. 121, from:

'Matthew: Ah! makes you feel bad, he does . . ' to p. 122, the middle of Matthew's speech:

'I never gave them a thought . . . the good he does.'

C Truth frees people from fear

Jesus showed that in God's Kingdom the standard was one of truth which involves absolute honesty. When talking to his disciples Jesus said, 'Beware of the leaven (teaching) of the Pharisees, which is hypocrisy. Nothing is covered up that will not be revealed, or hidden that will not be known. Whatever you have said in the dark shall be heard in the light, and what you have whispered in private rooms shall be proclaimed on the house-tops.' (Luke 12 : 1–3.) He told the Samaritan woman that God must be approached 'in spirit and in truth' (John 4 : 23).

Fear helped to kill Jesus. How? Read John 7 : 11–13.

Fear sometimes makes us dishonest. People can be dishonest about their faith through fear. But Jesus said, 'What I say to you in the dark you must repeat in broad daylight, what you hear whispered you must shout from the house-tops.' He went on to say, 'Do not fear those who kill the body, but cannot kill the soul. Fear him rather who can destroy both soul and body in hell.' (Matt. 10 : 27–28 – N.E.B.). Discuss what Jesus meant by the last sentence.

Fear gripped the disciples at Jesus' arrest so that they all fled, and Peter denied that he knew him. (Matt. 26 : 57, 69–70.)

For fear, the disciples met in secret in the upper room after Jesus' crucifixion, afraid to utter his name in public. (John 20 : 19.)

Research and questions

1. When did the disciples lose their fear and come out into the open to speak about Jesus? What gave them the power? *See* Acts 2.
2. What would have happened to Christianity if the disciples had not lost their fear and begun to speak out as apostles? Write down some of the things the world might have lost.
3. What do we call the people in the first three centuries A.D. who lost their lives because they dared to speak out about their faith?
4. Find out if there are still people today suffering for their faith. Name some if you can find out about them and tell their stories.
5. What kind of dishonesties does fear cause in people today?
6. 1 John 4 : 18 contains the phrase 'Perfect love casts out fear.' Fear can be a useful warning of danger, i.e. fear of being burnt by fire. Yet a mother out of love for her baby will go into a room which is on fire to rescue it. Give other examples of love overcoming fear.
7. Jesus said 'The truth shall make you free' (John 8 : 32). Sometimes small dishonesties and compromises can make people feel tied up inside. When they tell the truth, they experience a new freedom and can launch out in new ways because fear of people has gone.

EXAMPLE

As a young man William Booth was deeply stirred by the sufferings of the poor, the downtrodden, the outcast and the demoralised. He wanted to spend his life helping them, but he knew he must first get right with God. One thing stood in the way.

A few years before he had been able to help some school friends in a business matter. In gratitude they gave him a silver pencil-case. They thought he had done it just out of friendship; but actually he had made a profit for himself out of it. He knew he must tell them so. He didn't mind giving the case back, but he did mind admitting he had accepted it under false pretences. At last he decided and was honest with them.

After this he entered into his life's work and was able to help many thousands to get straight with God. Through the Salvation Army, which he founded, he futhered his aim to care for every last person in need.

Question

Why did William Booth feel it was so important that this matter must be put right?

D Faith or fear?

'Why are you afraid?' Jesus asked his disciples on one occasion. He expected them to have far more faith than they had. Look up the following instances and answer the questions:

Research and questions

1. Matt. 10 : 29–31. What was the reason Jesus gave for having no fear?
2. Luke 8 : 49–56. What caused Jairus's fear? What did Jesus tell him he needed instead of fear? Can we choose to have faith?
3. Luke 12 : 32. Jesus was talking to his disciples who had given up everything to follow him. Of what might they have been afraid?
4. Matt. 8 : 23–27. What did Jesus say when his companions expressed their fear?
5. Matt. 14 : 22–33. Peter demonstrated here how our thoughts of faith or fear affect our achievements. Of what was he thinking when he succeeded? When he failed? If possible give instances from life today.
6. Acts 27 : 24. This is an instance of one man's faith when most men feared. Paul was a prisoner, on the way to trial in Rome – a voyage full of danger, ending in shipwreck. Yet it was he who gave courage to all the others on the ship. Why?

E Fear or awe?

The word 'fear' is often used in the older versions of the Bible to mean 'awe' or 'reverence'.

Research and questions

1. Which of the following references to 'fear' in the Bible mean 'fear' and which mean 'awe'? (Use the Authorised Version of the Bible.) (*a*) John 7 : 13; (*b*) Matt. 28 : 8; (*c*) Acts 2 : 41–43; (*d*) 1 Peter 2 : 17. If you check these with the translations in the *New English Bible* you will know if you are right.
2. Do you think the fear Simon experienced in Luke 5 : 1–11 was good or bad for him? Give the reasons for your reply.
3. We read in Psalm 111 : 10 : 'The fear of the Lord is the beginning of wisdom.' Discuss this.

3 The Spirit of Love

Love and slavery

'I have come that people may have life and may have it in all its fulness' (John 10 : 10 – *N.E.B.*), said Jesus. Yet people sometimes ask, 'Doesn't being a Christian make you feel restricted?'

A good reply would be, 'Doesn't the warning by the edge of the cliff make you feel restricted? Why shouldn't you be allowed to fall over the edge?' Or, 'Why can't we drive on the wrong side of the road if we feel like it? That would be real freedom.' The question is, for how long – and for whom?

People have the queer idea that God wants to stop them enjoying themselves. Yet in the quotation above Jesus said the opposite. His aim was to give people the richest, fullest life possible.

Let us look at a few Christian lives:

Peter, Andrew, James and John were fishermen and likely to stay in the district around the Lake of Galilee for the rest of their lives. Then Jesus came along and within a few years they were travelling to many distant places, saying and doing things they never imagined possible.

Many Members of Parliament have lived, died and been forgotten. Yet Lord Shaftesbury and Wilberforce, who chose to dedicate their lives to fulfilling God's will instead of their personal ambitions, have been remembered down the ages for the great reforms which, as MPs, they achieved. Through their love and courage, they brought freedom to thousands who were slaves.

Florence Nightingale was well-to-do and might have lived a fairly idle life. But at the age of sixteen she had a call from God and was led into a strenuous life of heroic adventure. Her achievements in the Crimean War and the foundations she laid for good nursing and hospitals will never be forgotten.

Gladys Aylward was a servant and people said she had not the brains to become a missionary. But God had told her to go to China and so she saved up the money and went. She had amazing adventures there, including leading one hundred children in the historic march over the mountains out of peril into safety.

These are just a few from the many hundreds of people for whom Christianity has meant lives full and rich beyond their imaginings. They were prepared to follow Jesus and were not held back by circumstances or by being a slave to convention or other people's opinions. They went through hard and dangerous times, but thousands have benefited by their work.

For discussion

Did these experiences help to enrich their lives, and if so in what ways? NOTE: 'enrich', of course, has nothing to do with wealth.

Research and questions

1. Read Luke 4 : 16–21. Here Jesus quotes Isaiah 61 : 1 as describing what he has come to do – in fact, *is* doing. List the groups of people mentioned in verse 18 of Luke's quotation, and what Jesus was sent to do for each group: then write alongside each 'Restricting' or 'Releasing', whichever you think fits.
2. In today's world, who are the 'poor'? In what ways can there be 'good news' for them in all that Jesus brought to mankind?
3. In today's world, who are 'captives'? Name as many different types of captivity as you can think of, physical, mental, emotional and spiritual. To what was Zacchaeus a captive until Jesus freed him? Ask yourself: 'To what do I most easily fall captive?'
4. In today's world, who are the 'blind'? List other types of blindness besides loss of eyesight.
5. In today's world, who are 'oppressed'? And what by? Does anything 'oppress' you?
6. The MPs and women mentioned on page 41 did much to help the poor, the captives and the oppressed. Find out more about their adventures and the opposition they met. Who opposed them and why? What gave them the courage to go on despite reverses?

SOME SUGGESTED BOOKS

The People's Earl, M. St J. Fancourt (Longman) – Shaftesbury.
William Wilberforce, M.P., Oliver Warner (Batsford).
Brave Men Choose, G. D. Lean (Blandford) – chapters on Shaftesbury and Wilberforce.
Mr. Wilberforce, M.P., play by Alan Thornhill (Blandford).
Florence Nightingale, Cecil Woodham-Smith (Collins).
The Small Woman, Alan Burgess (Evans) – Gladys Aylward.
The London Sparrow, P. Thompson (Word Books) – Gladys Aylward.

B Love that changes people (Luke 7 : 36–50)

One day a Pharisee named Simon invited Jesus to dinner at his house. You know you have read a book properly and grasped what it describes if you can picture the scene and draw it or let it run through your mind like a film. The scene of this story is set in a flat-roofed house in the hot, dusty Middle East where manners and customs today are still much as they were in Jesus' day. A host who has invited a man as his guest goes to the door to meet him, and kisses him on both cheeks if he feels great respect or friendship for him, then taking his hands leads him indoors. They kick off their hot dusty shoes or sandals at the door; their bare feet are given a cool refreshing wash. Then they move into a shady room where they recline on couches with their feet up, a table in front of each with fruit on it, and, in very rich homes, a pool or even a fountain playing in the middle. Servants come and go behind the guests – some perhaps specially hired for the big occasion and so strangers to the household. They bring cool drinks.

Now you can picture the scene as Jesus comes to Simon's house and is taken through to the cool room where he and the other guests recline and talk until the meal is served – in the East the meal comes at the end of the visit, after the chat. How did Simon greet Jesus at the door? How much did he do to make sure his guest was comfortable? What sort of people do you think the other guests were? What could Simon's motive have been in asking Jesus to that house and that company in that way – a desire to learn? – to have it said by the neighbours 'Simon is entertaining the great teacher'? – to put Jesus in difficulties among enemies? – to do Jesus honour? – to give Jesus a rest, comfort, friendship and a good meal to encourage and strengthen him in his work? – or what? What might Jesus' motives have been in accepting?

Now you can see this woman slip in and move like one of the servants behind Jesus, break into tears over his poor tired hot dirty feet, then wipe off the dust of the road and the dampness of her weeping with her hair, and pour the expensive perfume she had brought with her over his feet – being too humble to pour it over his head as Eastern hosts do for their guests to this day. She was behind Jesus, at his feet.

It reads as if he had not yet looked at her. But Simon and the other guests could all see her: and knew her for what she was 'a woman of the streets and a sinner' (i.e. she made her living by prostitution). It is of course even possible that Simon had hired her to entertain his guests and to test Jesus, and that she was already in the house before the guests arrived, for Luke writes that she brought the ointment when she knew that Jesus was one of the guests. At any rate Simon started to say to himself, 'If this man were a prophet (as people say he is) he would have known what sort of a woman is touching him; for she is a sinner.'

Jesus looked at him and answered his thoughts with a request to speak. Simon replied, 'Teacher! speak on.' So Jesus told him a story, 'Once upon a time there were two men in debt to the same money-lender. One owed him £50 and the other £5. Since neither had anything to pay back with he generously cancelled the debt of each of them. Now, which do you suppose will love him more?'

'I suppose the one given the more generous favour,' replied Simon. 'You judged right,' said Jesus.

Then he looked at the woman (apparently for the first time through the whole event) and, pointing, said to Simon, 'You see this woman?' (He well knew that Simon and the others had been looking at her for some time.) Then he went on, 'I came into your house, you did not give me water on my feet: but she has rained tears on my feet and wiped them with the hair of her head. You gave me no kiss: but she has not stopped kissing my feet since I came in. You did not anoint my head with olive oil: but she has anointed my feet with perfume. I tell you that her sins which are many are forgiven for the reason that she loved much: but he loves little to whom little is forgiven.'

But to her he said, 'Your sins are forgiven.'

(It does not say whether this is the first time she has met Jesus and received forgiveness, or whether he had assured her of the forgiveness of her sins on some earlier occasion for which she was showing her gratitude.)

Then all those who were also reclining at the party like Jesus began to say to themselves: 'Who is this person who even forgives sins into the bargain?'

Jesus turned back to the woman and said, 'Your faith has saved you: go in peace!'

Research and questions

1. In what way did the woman put Simon to shame?
2. Can you guess at why she behaved in this way?
3. Compare Jesus' attitude to the woman and Simon's.
4. Men would creep to such a woman at night and make love, but would shun her and look respectable in the daytime. Jesus was not interested in visiting her at night. In fact he firmly showed her it was wrong. But he was not afraid to be seen talking to her in the daytime. Which of these was real love, and why? What is the word beginning also with 'l' shown by the other men?
5. Find another time when Jesus was brought into contact with a 'sinner' (a woman who had committed adultery). John 8 : 1–11. (In the *N.E.B.* it is at the end of John's gospel.) What did the scribes and Pharisees expect Jesus to say to her? What did he say to her?
6. Explain the meaning of the phrase 'Love the sinner, while hating the sin'. Do you think this a right attitude? Give reasons.

Love, marriage and divorce

Research and questions

1. What did Jesus say about marriage, divorce and sex outside marriage? Find out by reading Mark 10 : 11–12, Matt. 5 : 31–32 and Matt. 15 : 18–20.
2. Why did Moses, on some conditions, allow divorce?
3. What did Jesus say God intended about marriage when he created men and women?
4. What do the Ten Commandments say about adultery? Exodus 20 : 14.
5. Jesus said this was not enough. Read the part of the Sermon on the Mount where he talks about this. Matt. 5 : 27–28.
   Do you think he meant the same for women? Why do you think he said this?
6. Are the standards of Jesus higher or lower than those in the world today?
7. Try to find some recent figures on divorce from your library. What difficulties and unhappiness does divorce cause, and to whom?
8. What promise does this picture symbolise? Find the words of this promise in the Marriage Service and copy them out.

D   Love and Sex

Britain has been a great nation. It was through discipline and courage that men rose to great living. But during recent years we have been losing our greatness and some of our influence in the world has declined. Rome had the same experience. When she was at the peak of her splendour, there was much money to spend and moral standards weakened. As today, people began to try out all kinds of weird and strange ideas. Immorality and corruption began to take over. So Rome fell. Her influence had been great; the Western world had become more civilised because of her influence and as she declined men and women were afraid that civilisation would go too.

There was one thing which saved civilisation at the time of the fall of Rome. This was Christianity. The pagan peoples who conquered the lands of the former Roman Empire gradually became Christian, and left their heathen ways. It took a long time: the world went through dark days; but eventually pagan laws and cruelties changed and a more civilised society was established, because the invading pagans met Christians who were living a superior life which attracted and won many of them.

Augustine was one of the most powerful of these early Christians. Yet in his wild youth you would never have thought it possible. Later he was very unhappy that he had taken so long to be willing to accept the destiny God had for him. He wrote his *Confessions* in a book which has helped hundreds of other young men and women who have wanted to taste life's pleasures and not realised the emptiness and bitterness a self-willed life brings.

Augustine was the son of a well-to-do Roman civil servant in North Africa. Outwardly he lived a very gay life. When he was young he had a group of friends who felt that the most exciting way to live was to see how many forbidden things they could achieve. He always wanted to have more to boast about than anyone else. In this way he learned to give in to all his wrong desires and instincts. After a time he found himself a slave to these habits. Inside he was really miserable. He couldn't do without praise or women, and soon he had an illegitimate son. He loved his son, but the love was mingled with regret that he had not been born in the right circumstances. He began to want to find the truth about life. He was clever, but in spite of this he was not always successful with his pupils because he could not discipline himself.

He taught 'rhetoric', the art of public speaking, and was given a post in the imperial capital, Milan. There he went to hear the famous

Bishop Ambrose speak, to study his method. He took no notice of what was said, but only of the way it was said. Ambrose became his friend and brought him into touch with many Christians, whom he loved and admired. Increasingly he began to see that their way was right, but there was one big blockage which prevented him from following it. He couldn't face giving up his life with women. This had already ruined his chances of marriage. Underneath all his gaiety and cleverness, he was bitterly unhappy. He wanted the life Christ offered, but he was not willing to pay the price. He kept saying to God, 'Oh, Lord, make me pure, but not yet.'

One day a Christian friend called on Augustine and his companion, Alypius. He told them of a dedicated monk, Antony, whose story had so inspired two young men that they too had decided to put God first in their lives and give up material ambition. This made Augustine see how dirty and despicable his own life was.

When the friend left, he went off into the garden followed by Alypius. How free and happy were all those who were not slaves to their habits as he was! He felt so utterly ashamed and upset that he left Alypius and went off on his own.

Was there any way out of the conflict? Suddenly he heard a voice chanting a kind of song, 'Take and read. Take and read.' At first he thought it was children playing a game. Then he took it to be a command meant for himself. Going back to where Alypius was, he picked up a book he had put down earlier, the letters of Paul. He opened it and read the first passage which caught his eye:

> Let us live cleanly, as in the daylight; not in the 'delights', of getting drunk or playing with sex, nor yet in quarrellings or jealousies. Let us be Christ's men from head to foot, and give no chances to the flesh to have its fling.

As he read he realised he had at last decided. He would give over the direction of his life to God. What a relief that was! Quietly he told Alypius what had happened. Alypius was amazed to see him suddenly so different, calm and assured. Alypius asked what came next to the passage he had read. They looked together. 'Welcome a man whose flesh is weak . . .' This was exactly right for Alypius, who gave in too easily to what he knew was wrong. He said he was joining Augustine in his decision. Together they went in and told Augustine's mother. She had been praying for this for so many years. It was a wonderful moment for her.

Augustine found that he was worn out with his struggle. He gave up his university post and went away to think. He was no longer tempted and uncertain. A new strength began to grow in him, recognised by other people. He felt a love for all mankind. He began to write. It was then that he wrote his *Confessions* from which came the facts in this account. Many people came to him for help. In the end they persuaded him to become a priest and years later he was made Bishop of Hippo in Algeria, today called Bone, near the city where he was born.

During this time he went on writing. The Goths were overrunning Italy. They sacked Rome itself. Some people said it was because the Romans had deserted their gods. But Augustine wrote another book called *The City of God* in which he showed that earthly kingdoms rise and fall, but God's kingdom lasts for ever. This gave many people hope and courage to go on fighting to establish God's kingdom among the pagan victors and all over the world.

Augustine died as the Vandals broke into the walls of his own city, but his books were saved and lived on to help build the more permanent city of God. In that turbulent age Augustine had learnt and written: 'Thou hast made us for Thyself, and our hearts are restless until they find their rest in Thee.'

Research and questions

1. What started Augustine on his downward path?
2. What did he have to do before he was able to be free of the habits wrecking his life?
3. Read what Jesus says about getting rid of such habits: Matt. 5 : 29–30.
   (a) To what does he liken them?
   (b) How are we to get rid of them?

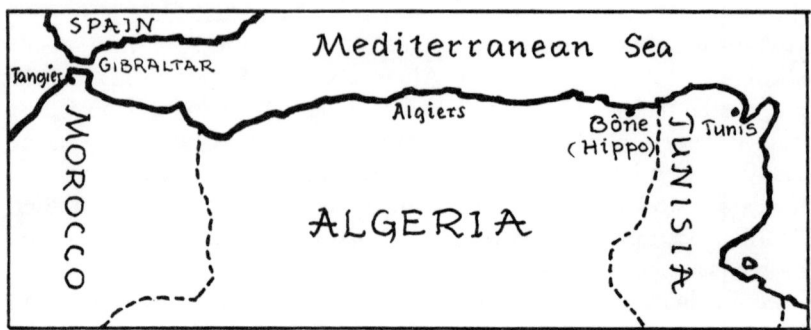

4. Find out about Augustine's mother, Monica. How far do you think her love and prayers for Augustine influenced his change?

5. The Greeks had four words to cover four different attitudes which we confuse by calling them all 'love'. Philía means friendship, storgé means caring, éros is sexual passion and agápe is selfless devotion. Which of these words would you expect to find in the New Testament describing the love of Jesus?

E Love and war

From all over the world come reports of wars and riots. At the time of writing there has been fighting in Vietnam for many years; India and Pakistan have been at war; in Northern Ireland violence and bloodshed have caused fear and destruction. Israelis and Arabs have been at one another's throats, Russia and China infringing one another's borders. There have been hijacking and assassination; many have gone in fear of their lives; thousands are homeless refugees. Yet everywhere there is a wish for peace.

Discuss and then write a short account of the state of the world as it is when you are taking these lessons. Illustrate with newspaper cuttings.

Also discuss the following questions:

How can we end wars? Do demonstrations against war help? Can we make laws against it? If so, what effect and value do they have? Has anyone yet found an answer?

Jesus had an answer long ago. It is simple to understand, but like all worthwhile things, far from easy to carry out. Where it has been tried it has been effective.

There were wars and riots in Jesus' day: Barabbas was a political prisoner as a riot leader. A party called the 'Zealots' was frequently starting insurrections in an attempt to get rid of the Romans, causing them endless trouble. Jesus apparently took no notice of all the political intrigues, and firmly refusing to be made a military leader, was quietly training his disciples to take a really radical answer to war across the world. Its basic principles are reported in the Sermon on the Mount.

Research and questions

1. Read these principles in Matt. 5 : 38–48, in a modern translation, such as that by J. B. Phillips. Remember that Jesus was thinking not so much of our outward actions as our inward attitude and thoughts.

NOTE: The first verse states a law Moses made years ago to prevent massive slaughter as reprisals for the injuries done to only one man. This law had been taken by the Jews as basic throughout all the centuries since, until Jesus showed this better way.

2. Did Jesus say, 'When anyone harms you do nothing'? If not, what did he tell them to do?

3. What do we normally want to do if anyone hurts us?

4. What do we feel inside?

5. Read Matt. 5 : 21–22. Discuss:

How possible is this attitude which Jesus commends: Do not let anger, resentment or bitterness turn you against the one who harms you. Keep open to him, even if he is likely to harm you again. Be ready to accept hurt if it comes?

Impossible? Only a saint could do that? A saint is just an ordinary human being like you or me, but he has decided to accept God's rule over every part of his life.

6. Jesus too shared our human nature. Did he do as he asked men to do? If so, on what occasions?

7. *For private thought:* Is there any resentment or anger I have against someone who I think has done wrong to me? Is there anything I should do about it?

8. Jesus said, 'Those who take the sword shall perish by the sword' (Matt. 26 : 52 – *R.S.V.*) Discuss this.

9. Some people today are turning to violence as a means to combat what they think is unjust or wrong, or as a way of life. Sometimes their motive may be to get their own back on society.

Discuss the following statement by Martin Luther King:

'Are we seeking for power's sake? Or are we seeking to make the world and our nation a better place? If we seek the latter, violence can never provide the answer. . . . Returning violence for violence multiplies violence. . . . Hate cannot drive out hate; only love can do that.' *Chaos or Community*, Martin Luther King, pp. 62–63.

10. Read the following poem and write it as a story.

YUSSOUF

A stranger came one night to Yussouf's tent,
Saying: 'Behold one outcast and in dread,
Against whose life the bow of Power is bent,
Who flies, and hath not where to lay his head.
I come to thee for shelter and for food:
To Yussouf, call'd through all our tribes the Good.'

'This tent is mine,' said Yussouf, 'but no more
Than it is God's: come in and be at peace;
Freely shalt thou partake of all my store,
As I of His who buildeth over these
Our tents His glorious roof of night and day,
And at whose door none ever yet heard nay.'

So Yussouf entertained his guest that night;
And waking him ere day, said: 'Here is gold;
My swiftest horse is saddled for thy flight.
Depart before the prying day grow bold!'
As one lamp lights another; nor grows less,
So nobleness enkindleth nobleness.

That inward light the stranger's face made grand
Which shines from all self-conquest; kneeling low,
He bow'd his forehead upon Yussouf's hand,
Sobbing: 'O Sheik! I cannot leave thee so. –
I will repay thee, – All this thou hast done
Unto that Ibrahim that slew thy son!'

'Take thrice the gold!' said Yussouf, 'for with thee
Into the desert, never to return,
My one black thought shall ride away from me.
First-born, for whom by day and night I yearn,
(Balanced and just are all of God's decrees),
Thou art avenged, my first-born! sleep in peace!'

James Russell Lowell

Further work

Arrange a reading of 1 Cor. 13 (J. B. Phillips' translation). Find and read true stories of where enemies have become reconciled.

SOME EXAMPLES

How to treat an enemy: *Readings for the School Assembly*, D. M. Prescott (Blandford), pp. 85–88.

Building unity between nations: 'A Woman of France' in *Man Alive*, J. & J. Kendall (Blandford), pp. 119-23.

The Price of Peace: *The Senior Teacher's Assembly Book*, D. M. Prescott (Blandford), pp. 126–27.

4 The Spirit of Unity

A Unity and personal differences

One of the problems of our age is communication. This is partly because the world has grown 'smaller' and many different people rub shoulders who would never have met in days gone by. Yet it is often the people nearest to us that we find hardest to talk to.

Research and questions (Nos. 1, 2 and 5 are for private thought)

1. Whom do you find it difficult to understand?
2. Who do you feel does not understand you?
3. Which groups of people in Britain\ seem to have little under-
   Which groups of people in the world∫ standing of one another?
4. There are various things we can do when we do not understand one another.

   Here are two of the most usual:

   (*a*) Decide to stay away from one another.

   (*b*) Clash, quarrel and fight until the winner imposes his ideas on the loser.

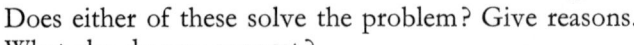

   Does either of these solve the problem? Give reasons. What else do you suggest?
5. St Francis of Assisi prayed:

   'may I seek
   Not so much to be comforted as to comfort
   To be understood as to show understanding'

How can I learn to understand the person I find most difficult?

B Unity and race differences

Much of Jesus' teaching is now separated from its original context. He may have used the same parables and sayings again and again. His disciples remembered them and collected them up after his death. Some of his teaching was directed to particular questions, and in the accounts of his life are recorded a number of his conversations. It is worth studying these to see how he dealt with people. Sometimes he made them answer his own questions. We are going to study in detail his conversation with the woman of Samaria recorded in John 4.

Samaria lay between Galilee and Judaea. The Jews and Samaritans had a deep-rooted quarrel which had lasted several hundred years. The Samaritans were of mixed race and mixed religion. The Jews believed that sacrifice should only be made to God in Jerusalem, and they had practised this since the days of Josiah in 621 B.C. The Samaritans however had built a temple on Mount Gerizim and they made sacrifices there. Jews and Samaritans had both treated each other badly in the past and they would not associate with each other. On one occasion when Jesus and his friends were travelling through Samaria, the Samaritans refused to give them lodgings. (Luke 9 : 51–53.)

Research and questions

Read carefully the conversation in John 4 : 1–42, and answer the following questions:

1. How many times did the woman say something quarrelsome?
2. How did Jesus react to each provoking remark?
3. How often did she change the subject? Why?
4. Do you ever act like this? Why?
5. What do you think Jesus meant in verses 10 and 14?
6. Why do you think he asked her to fetch her husband?
7. Did Jesus think of the woman as a Samaritan, or as a woman, or as a person in need?
8. What did he say both Jews and Samaritans needed?
9. Nowadays in many lands people of very different races, religions and backgrounds, have settled to live. Adjustment to this new and complex situation produces varied stresses and strains. The West Indian cricketer, Conrad Hunte, wrote of this:

Race is a fact of life. You were born white, yellow, brown or black. I was born black. We could not help it. Where we can help is to show that many races can learn to live and work together within a nation, beyond the differences of colour, creed, language and background. It can be done if we decide to do it.

After his years in professional cricket, latterly as vice-captain and opening bat of the West Indies team, Conrad Hunte has taken on as his main aim in life the task he outlines and is, as this book goes to press, touring Britain with a group to help bring about such collaboration and harmony in the major cities where people of mixed races most congregate.

You will find valuable material for your discussion in his book *Playing to Win*, Conrad Hunte (Hodder & Stoughton).

10. The opportunity of making a united world is now on our doorstep. Find out in what practical ways this opportunity is being taken, i.e. the BBC programme for immigrants on Sunday mornings 'Make yourself at home', technical assistance and training being given to students, what organisations such as the YWCA are doing, etc. How could we use this opportunity more?

Further work

The background to the quarrel between the Jews and Samaritans is given in:

2 Kings 17 : 24–34; Ezra 4 : 1–5; Nehemiah 4

You can find out how the disciples continued Jesus' work with the Samaritans in Acts 8.

SUGGESTED READING

An appropriate modern story is 'Relationships Matter Most' in *Readings for the Senior Assembly*, D. M. Prescott, p. 131.

In the same book, on p. 114, the extract from 'The Ascent of Everest' by John Hunt shows how unity among the Sherpas and others on the expedition lay behind its success.

C Unity and age differences

In the story of the Samaritan woman we saw how the difference of race or creed was really nothing to do with the woman's lack of understanding. It was the evil at the heart of her life which she was trying to cover up that made her appear unable to comprehend. Honesty brought understanding.

The age gap is often blamed for the lack of communication between parents and children. Here is a true modern story of how that gap was bridged.

David comes from Bootle. His home is in a terrace that runs down to the cranes and warehouses of the Mersey Docks. He is now nineteen years old, a passionate fan of the Liverpool Football Club and of Bob Dylan music. He plays a guitar, and now and then writes his own songs. His eye is bright, and his tongue has the lightning comeback he learned in street games and gang fights. If you hear him speak, you will know at once that David is a genuine Liverpool 'scouser'.

He works hard at his job as a painter. But his sights are on the future.

He is equipping himself, he says, to 'Do something effective to put things right in the world'. So he is training in public speaking, to write for newspapers, to study current affairs, and, as he puts it, to 'Deal with difficult people and change them'.

David was born in the country. His father was a postman in Ormskirk, his mother a landgirl, and their home a cottage on the farm where she worked. But when he was $10\frac{1}{2}$ years old, the family moved to Bootle. David remembers the shock of it. 'No fields. No cows. Only chimney stacks, dirty white-wash on the walls, clothes hanging on the lines, tom-cats at night.'

'At first', he says, 'the ladies in the shops used to say to my mother, "How nice David is!" They admired my country manners and my short pants. But gradually they stopped saying it, as I grew like the other boys: scars on my face, football in the street, being chased, setting off bangers.'

'I never told my parents if I got into trouble at school', David says. 'Never, never admitted I'd been in a fight. That's where the generation gap in our family began. I didn't want them to find out that their son was not the smashing guy they thought he was.' Money was short, and his mum had to go out to work. When he came home from school, David hated sometimes having to find food for himself and clean up the mess the cat had made.

Then the family had to move, twice – first to the country, then back to Bootle. It meant a double change of schools for David and a double postponement of his O-levels. 'I resented my dad making us move like that just because he would have a better job', says David. 'I thought, "He's had a good life. It's my turn now".' He began to lose interest in his books.

Soon he began to mix with the lads who went to the off-licence houses, drinking, going out with the girls: 'I never told my mum and dad about them.' Instead, he lied about what he did.

Back in Bootle, he enrolled at 'The Tech'. There he was elected to the Students' Representative Council and took part in 'student power' action.

Pop festivals, ale-house parties and football matches filled his life. Though he passed six O-levels, he was more interested in the girls he picked up most nights. Then he himself got picked up – by the police, outside Liverpool's 'Cavern', the night-spot where The Beatles first hit the charts. The police phoned his parents. When David came home, a furious dad and mum confronted him. The gap between his parents and himself yawned like a chasm.

What dug that gap? David has his diagnosis clear. First, there was the dishonesty that made the three of them wear masks: 'We were three split personalities, pretending to be what we were not.' Then division bred division: 'My mum used to side with me against my dad – and then I would get mad with both of them.' Finally, there was fashion. His dad tried hard to keep David's friendship, going long nature walks with him. But fashion decreed that fathers and sons must not be seen together outside the home. So the two of them had to travel by different routes and meet outside the district, when they wanted to go anywhere together. 'I wanted to be pally with my dad. But I wanted to be "in" with my mates. I found I couldn't mix the two.'

Today David is equally outspoken in describing how he and his parents have closed the gap. 'Honesty and a common aim did it', he says.

The aim came first. On the invitation of a former teacher, he went for a weekend to the Moral Re-armament Conference Centre at Tirley Garth in Cheshire. 'There I met a crowd', he says, 'Young and old, and from all kinds of backgrounds and countries, who were moving faster than me and my friends, and knew where they were going.' David caught from them a growing Christian faith and a way of living it 'not watered down but speaking out'. It was something he had stopped thinking about since he was thrown out of the Church choir for fighting in the pews. He learnt how to find God's direction for his life. 'My generation could solve so many of the problems of the world if we became guided by God', he says. 'It needs the strength of the young, as well as the wisdom of the old, to build a better society.'

Honesty was the first, tough step David took on this new road. He told his parents the truth. All he had hidden from them came out into the light. They began to do the same with him. 'That day my dad and I began to talk as men. He was no longer a lecturer, trying to teach me. We found there was no generation gap, only an honesty gap. And we closed it.'

Here is his own conclusion. 'The answer is not for the Vicar to grow long hair, wear flowered shirts and play an electric guitar. Nor is it for the hippy to get a "short back and sides", wear a bowler and a black suit and carry a briefcase. The younger generation complains at the negative lead, if any at all, that is given to us by the older generation. But we cannot expect to be led along all our lives. We need to stand up straight, look around, find the right course, and march steadily on it. We can lead – and at such a pace that everybody moves faster. We need to be responsible for a new generation ourselves in years to come. We need honest relationships, purity in and out of marriage, unselfishness and love in all walks of life. If we all did try and live this way, we would find the gap close, and young and old would be equal under God. And we would find the sparkling glow of a fresh, moving purpose.'

Henry Macnicol

Research and questions

1. What caused the generation gap in David's family, and where did it start?
2. How was it closed, according to David. What did he do towards this? What did his parents do?
3. From this story, would you say the basic cause of a generation gap is difference of age or that other factors are largely responsible? Explain.
4. What does David say is needed to build a better society?
5. What do you think would happen to many of the divisions of the world if statesmen and ordinary people of all races began to be honest with one another like this? Why do you think as you do?
6. 'For he is our peace who hath made us both one, and has broken down the dividing wall of hostility' wrote Paul, the Jew, to the Gentiles of Ephesus (Eph. 2 : 14, R.S.V.).
   (*a*) What did it cost Jesus to make this possible?
   (*b*) What did it cost David and his parents to break down the walls between them?
   (*c*) Which cost more – the old division or the new unity?
7. Write down any other thoughts that come to you.

Section III

A NEW SOCIETY–PEOPLE GOVERNED BY GOD

1 On What is Your Life Built?

A Good foundations

A visitor was shown a marvellous new hospital, which had been badly needed in the district. She admired it very much. Then a friend said,

'If you were able to look more closely, you would see that it has great cracks already appearing in some of the walls, which will make it unfit for use.'

'Whatever has caused them?'

'Subsidence. There's a coal-mine under the site. The surveyors didn't make sure the tunnelled rock was strong enough to carry this large building. So all those thousands of pounds are wasted – and worse, thousands of patients will have to wait for treatment.'

What story in the Bible does this remind you of?

Research and questions

1. The story in the Bible is at the end of Matthew's account of Jesus' Sermon on the Mount. It gives Jesus' main point in all he has been saying. Find the story. Write as a title 'The Two Houses' and put the Bible reference.
2. This parable is about the foundations on which we build our lives.
   (*a*) To whom does Jesus compare the wise man? Make sure you copy *all* the words in the applicable phrase.
   (*b*) To whom does he compare the foolish man?
   (*c*) What was the difference between them?
3. On whose words do we build our lives? Name some of the people whose training goes into building our characters.
4. Do you agree that some of this training comes from books? If so, can you name some books which have given you the ideas you live by?
5. From what other sources do the ideas come which form our characters?
6. Name some sources which sometimes give us the wrong ideas.
7. How far can we blame these sources for our bad characteristics?

Remember we have been given a power of choice. Give reasons for your answer.

8. The power of choice is the free-will to decide how we will live our lives. What basis for living does Jesus say a wise man decides to choose? Matt. 7 : 24.

3   Standing the test

The story of the two houses tells of how they stood the test. Here is the story of how the faith of two women stood the test. They are true stories.

Carol was a singer. She had faith in God and used it in doing his work. Quite suddenly she developed an illness called disseminated sclerosis. She soon found what a terrible disease this is. It gradually took away the use of her limbs and she became more and more helpless. This loss of control affected her speech and she could no longer give pleasure with her singing. After years of getting gradually worse she had to spend most of her time in bed and became utterly dependent on others. You can imagine her misery and sense of uselessness.

She had learnt the secret of conversation with God (sometimes called 'communing with God'). This meant she did not just talk to God in her prayers, only asking for things, but listened to what he had to say to her, too. Some years before she was ill she had decided to do his will and let her life be directed by him, and she meant to stand by this decision whatever happened. Her illness was the test.

She continued having these conversations with God and during one of these quiet times with him an interesting thought came. 'You can be of more use to me as you are,' he seemed to be saying, 'than you ever could have been when you were well.'

From then on she had a purpose in life, and many people have been helped in their visits to her. They see her appreciative and hopeful, full of an interest in their affairs and in everything beyond her four walls. They have come away realising how small are their causes for grievance in comparison with hers. If she could be as outgoing as that, they could surely give up their own self-centred moanings.

* * *

Ann was a mother. She went to church and professed a faith in God. Then, tragically, she lost her son, and was utterly shattered. Nothing seemed to help her. She blamed God, left the Church and gave up her faith. She became bitter and resentful about everything and everyone and was a great trial to live with from that time onwards. No one who met her found help for their troubles, but only a greater sense of burden.

Research and questions

1. What decision had Carol made which enabled her to 'weather the storm' triumphantly?
2. Read Matt. 7 : 21. What did Jesus say was the most important thing God asks of us?

Further work

Much of what we have been studying so far has been based on Jesus' Sermon on the Mount.

Read through Matt. 5, the first chapter of the Sermon on the Mount, and write down any thoughts or questions you have on this. This may lead to further discussion with your teacher.

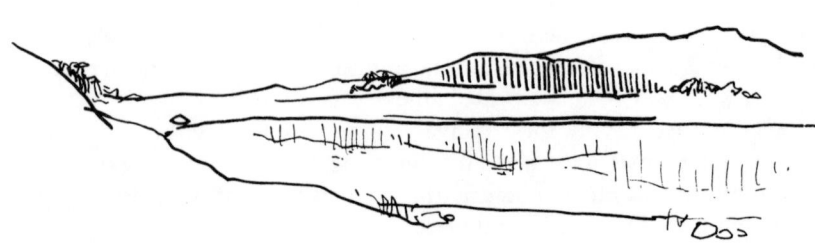

2 What Are You Governed By?

We may not worship idols today, as many did in the Old Testament, but we often have 'gods' which we set up for ourselves. In this section we shall discover what some of these are.

A The 'god' of material possessions

Discuss as a class the following questions:

1. What is the first of the Ten Commandments? (Exodus 20: 3).
2. Read Luke 12 : 16–21 – the story of the rich fool as told by Jesus. What did the rich man make his 'god'? How did his 'god' let him down and show himself to be a false one?
3. What other 'gods' do people have today?
4. Find the following phrase in the verses you have just read, 'a man's life does not consist . . .'. (R.S.V.) Read the rest of the sentence.
5. Of what else does life consist? What really makes us happy and satisfied?

Research and questions

1. Write out the phrase in question 4 above, completing the sentence.
2. Read Matt. 19 : 16–25. Was the rich young ruler a good man or a bad one? Give reasons for your answer.
3. In what way was the rich young ruler like the rich fool? What did they both put first in their lives?
4. What did Jesus promise the rich young ruler if he would dare to give up his material security and put his trust in God?
5. What did Jesus tell his disciples would be the result for anyone who gave up everything for his sake?
6. Turn back to Luke 12 : 33–34. In what way is this 'treasure in heaven' better than material security? Put this in your own words.
7. Do people put their trust in material possessions today? Give examples. Can you think which of the world's troubles are caused by this?

B Other 'gods'

In the last assignment the people we discussed made a god of their possessions. People choose many other gods. You and I and every human being have an inner life as well as an outer one.

We have thoughts, feelings and inner experiences. We sometimes feel turbulent inside, miserable, full of jealousy, bitterness, hurt or longing – or happy, at peace, or full of excitement, or of goodwill and love for others; sometimes 'up' and sometimes 'down'. It is here in our inner lives that we choose the gods we will follow. Often we make our feelings our gods. Here are some examples:

1. If we like feeling safe we avoid danger, and if we let fear rule us, security becomes our god.
2. If we let the thrill of success control us, we avoid doing what is right if we are likely to fail.
3. As we have seen with Augustine, if we let sex feelings get a grip on us we say they are necessary and must be indulged. They have become our god. Instead of trying to find freedom from being controlled by them so that their use in family life at the right time is a precious gift, we look instead for ways of avoiding trouble. The world is full of the sad results of such a god in control.
4. Continual excitement can become our god so that we are never happy alone or when life is quiet. This is usually a sign of a deeper unrest and dissatisfaction.
5. We may let bitterness become our master and sour our lives and spread our misery to others.
6. We often make people our gods – because we like them to be pleased with us or we fear their displeasure. This happens with friends, parents, husbands, wives or children.

For private thought: Which of the above examples are apt to be my gods? Have I other gods not mentioned here?

For discussion

St Augustine said: 'Thou hast made us for Thyself, and our hearts are restless until they find their rest in Thee.' What connection does this have with this assignment?

C   The guidance of God

Many times a person guided by God has started a revolutionary train of events which has affected history. The person simply obeyed a prompting of God without any idea of where it would lead. The early Christians were said to have 'turned the world upside down'. (Acts 17 : 6). Peter was one of these. Sometime after the first Whitsun, he was guided by God to stay at the home of Simon a tanner in Joppa. There he had a vision of God asking him to break the thousands-of-years-old Jewish tradition of not eating certain meats. 'What God has cleansed, you must not call common' (unclean). This set him thinking. Not only meats, but also Gentiles, were 'unclean' to the Jews.

Then came a knock on the door. Three Gentiles were looking for him. With a sense that they would ask him something unusual, but that he need have no fear in conceding it, he went to meet them. They asked him to go thirty miles north with them to the home of a leading Roman in Caesarea, a centurion who had some appreciation of the Jewish faith, and wanted to talk to him. Peter asked some of the Christians from Joppa to accompany him, and they did so. Peter followed through the guidance God had given him, even though it seemed to go against what he had previously thought and might bring disapproval from fellow Jews. As a result the Roman centurion and his family became Christians. Peter's act of obedience opened the door for the faith in Jesus Christ to spread beyond the confines of the small Jewish community. It was now open to everyone, everywhere. From this beginning the Christian faith grew and spread across the world and down the centuries, radically changing our history and shaping our lives and culture even more than we are able to realise.

Research and questions

1. Read of Peter's vision and the result in Acts 10, and of how he had to answer for his behaviour before his fellow Jews in the Christian community. *See* Acts 11 : 1–18.
2. All the great leaders of the Old Testament felt that God's will was the most important thing in their lives. Here are two examples.
   (*a*) Read Genesis 26 : 25 and write down what Isaac did first when he settled in Canaan to establish the new nation there. What would people without faith in God have done first?
   (*b*) When Goliath threatened Israel what do you think would have happened if David had not turned up? What did David have which the other men of Israel had not? Copy out 1 Sam. 17 : 45.
3. The Acts of the Apostles is the story of how Jesus' followers started the revolution of bringing in Christ's New Society, by letting God guide them step by step. One man who obeyed needed courage to do so. Jesus' followers in Damascus were awaiting, in fear, the arrival of their persecutor, Saul. Ananias received a surprising direction from God. Find out what it was from Acts 9 : 11. Read on to discover Ananias' reaction. What would a man with less faith and courage have done? When Ananias dared to obey, what was the result – not only for Saul, but later for the world?

SOME MODERN EXAMPLES OF GOD'S GUIDANCE ARE TO BE FOUND IN

God's Smuggler, Brother Andrew (Hodder & Stoughton).
The London Sparrow, P. Thompson (Word Books).
Readings for the Senior Assembly, D. M. Prescott (Blandford).
Senior Teacher's Assembly Book, D. M. Prescott (Blandford) – the section
  'True Stories of the Present Day'.

D Two-way prayer

Which of the following makes the best kind of companion?
  Someone who does all the talking?

  Someone who is always asking you to do things but never taking
any interest in what you might want or need?
  Someone who listens to you as well as talking himself?
  Someone eager to join in with your suggestions as well as to proffer
ideas of his own?
  Have you ever thought of the way many people treat God? Which
of the above four ways is most usual?
  How did Jesus pray?
  We have seen Jesus at prayer at his baptism. His time in the wilderness, when he was being tempted, was also a time of prayer. As he
struggled to find the right way to do God's work, he looked for God's
thoughts to answer the wrong ones the devil was trying to put into
his mind. This is part of prayer.
  Many people down the ages have had a kind of prayer-struggle
before they have seen or accepted God's way. David Wilkerson in his
book *The Cross and the Switchblade* (Hodder & Stoughton) tells of such
a prayer-struggle before he accepted God's orders to go into the worst
areas of New York to help drug-taking youth.

Research and questions

1. Read *The Cross and the Switchblade*, Chapter 1, or another account of a struggle in prayer to find God's will.
   Write the title of your reading and a short summary of its content.
2. There were many times when Jesus sought God's guidance. Luke especially seemed interested in Jesus at prayer and records several instances. Look up the following references and make a note on the problems Jesus apparently had to solve, where and how he prayed, and the decisions he arrived at.
   (*a*) Luke 4 : 40–44 (also recorded in Mark 1 : 32–39).
   (*b*) Luke 6 : 12–16.
3. Read John 14 : 13–14. What do you think prayer 'in my name' means? To the Jews, the name represented the character of the person. How should this affect the kind of things we pray for?
4. One important reason for prayer is to get in line with God's thinking. This often entails change in ourselves, in our demands and desires. Then we find ourselves asking for the right things.
   Read about an important occasion when Jesus needed prayer for this reason: Matt. 26 : 36–46. What was Jesus' human wish? How did prayer help him?

Further work

1. Read further examples of Jesus at prayer. Where did he pray on each occasion, and what was the purpose?
   Luke 6 : 12–13;   9 : 16;   9 : 18, 28;   10 : 21;   23 : 34, 46.
2. What did Jesus teach about prayer on the following occasions?
   Matt. 6 : 5–15, Luke 11 : 1–13, Luke 18 : 1–14, Matt. 18 : 19–20.
3. Prayers for forgiveness: Read the following parables and say what each teaches about forgiveness
   (*a*) The Unmerciful Servant, Matt. 18 : 21–35.
   The Pharisee and the Publican, Luke 18 : 9–14.
   (*b*) God's response: The Lost Sheep
   　　　　　　　　　The Lost Coin　　} Luke 15.
   　　　　　　　　　The Prodigal Son

Section IV

TRAINING A FORCE FOR THE NEW SOCIETY

1 Great Expectations

A Choosing a team

If you were choosing a team to play a football or a hockey match you would choose those who were best at playing that game. Jesus' team do not seem to have been best at anything. They were a most ordinary group of people, all very different. Four were fishermen used to a tough, open-air life. One was a white-collar worker who spent his time in an office. A sixth was a member of a revolutionary movement, the Zealots, out to get rid of the Roman occupiers of their country, if necessary by violence. There were six others, making twelve disciples (or apostles) in all – including three pairs of brothers.

In spite of their differences there was one thing they had in common. They were all so struck by what they had seen of Jesus that they were ready to leave everything, homes and families, jobs and livelihood, all known forms of security, to go with him wherever he took them. Surely if they could have seen the results down the ages affecting lands they did not even know existed, they would have been utterly bewildered and astonished. They were certain Jesus was going to lead them to something great, but their ideas did not go beyond their own nation, the Jews.

Research and questions

1. Name the six disciples first mentioned above, explaining which was which. Luke 6 : 12–16.
2. One of the first things a sports team has to do is to learn to play together. One of the first things the twelve had to do was to learn to live together. Which two of the above six, do you think, might have found it most difficult to accept one another? Why?
3. Do you think most of the twelve would have been used to accepting invitations such as the one mentioned in Mark 2 : 14–17? Why do you give this answer? What would they learn from participating in this event?
4. Which people would you never expect to give you an invitation to a meal? Why would you feel embarrassed if you were so invited?

5. What happens to the work of a team if some of the members do not get on well together?

Team-work?

Watching, learning, helping

If you are learning a new job, at first you may have to follow your instructor around, watching what he does and listening to instructions, helping where you can. This was the twelve disciples' programme for some time, in fact for most of Jesus' three years of work before his crucifixion. We have heard much of what the disciples saw him doing, and heard him teaching.

Research and questions

1. What would the disciples have learnt from the event told in Matt. 19 : 13–14.
2. How did the disciples help on the occasion described in Mark 6 : 30–44?
3. Whose boat was perhaps used when Jesus was teaching as described in Mark 4 : 1?
4. In what other ways did the disciples aid Jesus in his work by the use of their boats? Mark 3 : 9, Mark 6 : 32 and 53.
5. Name one parable they heard him tell. They obviously remembered them well. Why? Because they are vivid stories – because they told them often to others themselves – or for what other reasons?
6. Why do you think the parables and sayings are written in a different order in each gospel?
7. In learning your instructions for a new job, you would have to ask

some questions. What questions did the disciples ask Jesus in
(a) Mark 4 : 10 and (b) Mark 9 : 28? Look back in each case to see
what the question was about.

C Facing fear and opposition

In following Jesus, the disciples had many unexpected things to face.
Jesus used everything that happened as an opportunity for training.
He taught them how to deal with fear and with opposition.

Research and questions

1. Notice the points of training
   in the episode of the storm on
   the lake, Matt. 8 : 23–27, and
   answer the following questions:
   (a) Did Jesus save the dis-
       ciples from facing disaster?
   (b) What did their own failure
       lead them to do?
   (c) What did Jesus say to
       them when the storm was
       over?
   (d) What would they learn
       from all this?

2. Do you find criticism and opposition easy to face? The disciples
   would be meeting a very great deal of this in the future. One of the
   earliest criticisms came when Matthew (Levi) was giving his re-
   ception for Jesus to meet his friends. Read Mark 2 : 14–17.
   (a) What question did the Pharisees ask in criticism?
   (b) Of whom did they ask it?
   (c) Notice that the disciples faced the criticism alone first, and then
       Jesus came forward with the answer. What was it?

D Trying it out

There comes a point in training where you have to try it out for
yourself – like a college student on teaching practice. Will you be able
to do it? You have a sense of excitement and nervousness. You may
wonder how the twelve felt as Jesus told them he was sending them
out for the first time into the villages to preach the Good News and
to heal.

Research and questions

1. Which verse in Luke 9 : 1–6 shows the training that Jesus was now giving them in living by faith in God and not in any worldly possessions?
2. What does Luke tell us they were able to do?
3. There were, of course, many other disciples besides the twelve who followed Jesus. Luke gives an account of Jesus sending out seventy disciples in a similar way. Read Luke 10 : 1–11 and Luke 10 : 17–20.
   (*a*) What was the result of the mission of the seventy?
   (*b*) What did Jesus mean by his warning in Luke 10 : 20?
4. There are many instances where men and women who have undertaken to venture forth for God have learnt to make him their only security. Write of any example you know.

SUGGESTED EXAMPLES

These may be found in:
God's Smuggler, Brother Andrew (Hodder & Stoughton).
Dr Barnardo, Norman Wymer (Longman).
George Muller and his Orphans, N. Garton (Longman).

E Success

The disciples were excited with the way their expectations had been fulfilled. They needed a rest, and Jesus intended them to have one. They were also ready for the next step in training – that success was not the main aim, but something else.

Research and questions

1. What happened to prevent the disciples having a rest after their hard work? Luke 9 : 11–17. What was Jesus' attitude to the interruption? What would ours be?
2. Read what the crowds tried to do to Jesus in John 6 : 15. What was it?
3. Why did this perturb Jesus?
4. What did he do?

2   A Different Kind of Leader

A   'Who do men say that I am?'

At the end of the last assignment we learned that Jesus withdrew to the hills because the people wanted forcibly to make him king. Perhaps he was praying up in the hills as to what to do next. He knew he was not going to be that kind of king. Very soon after, he took the twelve out of Palestine into the country in the north, to a place called Caesarea Philippi where he could talk to them alone.

Read Luke's account of what happened there, Luke 9 : 18–20. What was Jesus trying to find out?

As soon as Jesus knew that the disciples had come to believe him to be the promised Messiah, the one they expected to be king, he began to show them how different that kingship was to be from all they had imagined.

Research and questions

1. Read Luke 9 : 21–22. What was the difference between the disciples idea of Jesus' Messiahship and what Jesus was telling them here?
2. This was a great shock to the twelve. Mark tells us something Luke does not give which shows us how disturbed the disciples were by what Jesus told them. Read Mark 8 : 31–33. What did Peter do?
3. What do you think Jesus meant by his very stern reply to Peter?
4. What events do you think led Jesus to see the end of his life on earth in this way?
5. There are four poems in Isaiah 42 : 1–9; 49 : 1–12; 52 : 13–15; 53 : 1–12 which speak of 'The Suffering Servant' as the one sent by God. Jesus was familiar with the Scriptures and would also know from these that it was not as an earthly king but as a Servant suffering for his people that he would conquer men's hearts, and so fulfil the prophecy. Read Isaiah 53 : 1–12.
6. Was it Jesus alone who was to expect suffering? Read Mark 8 : 34–37. Try to put this passage into your own words. If you find it difficult, discuss it first with your teacher.
7. These were such revolutionary ideas that the disciples were a long time taking them in. One thing that Jesus said they do not seem to have noticed at first. What was this? Mark 8 : 31, the last six words.
8. Jesus went on repeating this prophecy of his death and resurrection. It became the basis of his next phase of training for the disciples from then on. Look up the references in Mark where he repeated

this information: Mark 9 : 30–32, Mark 10 : 32–34. Where were Jesus and the twelve in each instance? Why did Jesus try to pass through Galilee unnoticed? Mark 9 : 30.
9. Imagine two of the puzzled disciples discussing this news from Jesus. Write a short conversation they might have had about it.

B 'Listen to Him'

Jesus shared with his three most intimate disciples an experience which gave them confidence that they were right in believing him to be the promised Messiah, the Christ. This was an event which they would never forget. Mark says this happened six (Luke, 'about eight') days after the events at Caesarea Philippi.

Read Mark 9 : 2–9. What do we call this experience?

The Jewish Scriptures were made up of the Law and the Prophets. Moses stood for the Jewish Law and Elijah for the Prophets. To see them together with Jesus showed that they were in accord. The words the disciples heard from the cloud told them to 'Listen to him'; his teaching fulfilled the best on which the Jews had been basing their lives until this time and took them the next step.

Research and questions

1. Were the disciples to tell everyone about their experience? Why do you think Jesus gave the order in Mark 9 : 9?
2. Read Mark 10 : 32–45. The disciples were slowly beginning to understand something of what Jesus was saying. Which words in Mark 10 : 32 show this?
3. Yet how little was the understanding of two who had even been on the Mount of Transfiguration is shown by Mark 10 : 35–37. Who were the two and how did they show they still thought of Jesus as an earthly king?
4. Jesus reminded them again of the kind of king he was to be. Which words in Mark 10 : 38 show this? What did Jesus mean by these words, and by those in Mark 10 : 39? Read on to verse 40.
5. Having reminded them that he was to be the Suffering Servant, he went on to tell them who were to be the greatest in his kingdom. Who were to be the greatest there? Mark 10 : 41–45.
6. Can you understand the feelings of the other ten disciples as reported in Mark 10 : 41? If you had been one of them, do you think that after Jesus' words in verses 41–45 you would have felt rather small? If so, why?

Section V

THE COST OF THE NEW SOCIETY

1 What is Right, Not What is Safe

A Conflict and opposition

Jesus saw much need for change in the leadership of his nation. In his day the leadership lay with the priests, scribes and lawyers.* The religious life these men had established for the Jews was perhaps the best in the world at that time. It was admired by many. Jesus did not want to destroy it, only to deepen its meaning. In it lay the foundations of the new society – God's kingdom. But the leaders interpreted the Law in their own way and narrowed it down. They wanted to keep everything under their control, and felt that Jesus threatened their position.

Have you met any who want to keep everything exactly as it is – who resent anyone else making suggestions? Perhaps you know of a gang leader who won't let anyone join his group unless they accept his leadership. Can you think of reasons why people are like this?

Because the Pharisees and Sadducees resented Jesus' arrival they looked for every possible occasion to trip him and his disciples up and to say that they were not keeping the Law as laid down by Moses.

Research and questions

1. Read Mark 2 : 1 to 3 : 6. List the criticisms made against Jesus in this passage. Find other instances in Matt. 9 : 3 and Luke 11 : 37–38 and add them to your list.
2. Why do you think the Pharisees and scribes criticised Jesus?
3. When people who matter criticise what you do, do you:
   (*a*) try to act from then on as they would want?
   (*b*) react angrily in self-defence?   (*c*) or what?
4. Did Jesus change his actions to suit authority? Or react in self-defence? Or whom was he concerned to please?

   To answer this question read Jesus' reply to the Pharisees who complained that he did not wash ceremonially before his meals (not a matter of hygiene), Luke 11 : 39–44.

* They belonged to two rival political parties: the Pharisees and the Sadducees. The Pharisees wanted nationalist separation; the Sadducees sought national survival in a measure of co-operation with the Roman occupying power.

5. Read Luke 11 : 53–54. Put in your own words what the scribes and Pharisees were now beginning to do.
6. Mark 3 : 6 shows how the Pharisees' criticisms had grown into something far more ugly. What was that?

3 The road of triumph

Earlier we read of Jesus preparing his disciples for what he and they were soon to face. They were on their way south to Jerusalem. Crowds of people were on the road, on the other side of the River Jordan, avoiding the unfriendly Samaritan area. They were in holiday mood, going up to Jerusalem for the Passover, travelling in families and larger groups for safety. Chasing about among them would be children, particularly boys of twelve, the age at which they went to their first Passover, as young adults. There would be laughter, singing and endless chatter.

Jesus was recognised and besieged by the crowds from Galilee. He taught and healed – and in quieter moments found time to give his closest followers new warnings of what was to come. Luke tells us they still did not understand.

The gospels record that on the way the Pharisees came up and tried yet again to get evidence against him by asking test questions about divorce. They wanted to see if he held unorthodox views which they could quote against him.

John 11 : 55–57 says that Jews in Jerusalem were speculating whether Jesus would dare to come to the Passover, for both the chief priests (Sadducees) and the Pharisees had given orders that anyone who knew where Jesus was should let them know, so that they might arrest him.

The disciples sensed that something was going to happen. For them the journey was tinged with fear, and at the same time excitement (Mark 10 : 32). Would Jesus at the last moment show himself to be truly the Messiah and outwit his enemies? Was he to become king and bring in his kingdom during Passover week? It was a fitting occasion.

Research and questions

1. Now, surprisingly, Jesus himself chose to act as a king, something he had refused to allow others to force him to do.

    Read again the account of his triumphal entry into Jerusalem from any of the gospels. You will find it in Luke 19 : 28–40.

Do you think it appears that Jesus had made an earlier arrangement with someone about the use of his colt? What leads you to your conclusion?

2. Turn to Zechariah 9 : 9. This was a prophecy from the Jewish Scriptures foretelling the coming of the Messiah. What do you think Jesus was doing deliberately by this action, in what was to be the last week of his life and the last time he was to enter Jerusalem freely? (In Matthew's account this prophecy is quoted.)

3. Which verse in Luke 19 shows you that the people knew the prophecy and what it must mean about Jesus?

4. Why did the Pharisees want Jesus to rebuke his disciples and followers?

5. What was Jesus' reply, and what did he mean?

6. When pilgrims came in sight of Jerusalem they often wept with pride at the glorious sight of the city and its Temple glittering in the sun. They frequently burst into song.

    Jesus also wept, but for a different reason. Luke 19 : 41–44. He saw beyond the pride and glitter. What did he foresee for the city? Find out when this prophecy actually came true.

7. Jesus exclaimed, 'Would that even today you knew the things that make for peace!' (Luke 19 : 42.) What did he mean?

8. On entering Jerusalem as its king (that same evening according to Matthew and Luke, but next morning according to Mark), Jesus performed another action as Messiah. What was that? Luke 19 : 45–46.

9. Jesus' words in the Temple were, again, quotations from the Jewish Scriptures. Look up Isaiah 56 : 7 and Jeremiah 7 : 11. Jesus recalled the prophet Jeremiah's similar charge of six hundred years earlier. What was taking place now to cause Jesus to make this condemnation?

10. Think of the feelings of the twelve. Here was Jesus in great danger, yet apparently doing everything to get himself into worse trouble. Why do you think he did it?

11. (*a*) What was the reaction of the authorities? Luke 19 : 47. (*b*) Was it surprising? (*c*) Why did they feel helpless? (*d*) In the meantime, what did Jesus continue to do?

2 The Twisters

Jesus' actions in riding into Jerusalem as the Messiah-King, and in showing his authority in the Temple, had made the Jewish leaders so angry that all they wanted to do was to destroy him.

Unable to do so because of his popularity with the crowds, they held meetings to think together what to do. By Tuesday, according to Mark, they had planned to send different groups of people to him with test questions. These were designed to trick him into saying something so unorthodox and shocking that even the crowds would turn against him. If that did not work, the questions might bring treasonable answers which they could repeat to the Roman authorities, so that the Romans would have him put to death. The questions were carefully put so that Jesus would be in trouble however he answered them – or so they thought.

Three of the questions Jesus was asked can be found in:

Mark 11 : 27–33; Mark 12 : 13–17; Mark 12 : 18–27

By whose authority?

Mark 11 : 27–33

Research and questions

1. What was the first question? Who asked it?
2. Jesus answered by asking them a question in return. What was it?
3. Why did the questioners find it hard to answer Jesus' question without getting *themselves* into trouble?
4. What was Jesus' final reply?
5. Do you think this was clever of Jesus? If so, why?
6. What was Jesus trying to get them to understand by his answers?
7. Can you think of any equivalent trick-questions which might be put to Jesus today, say by a television interviewer or press reporter, to try to make him take sides or express a political or sectional opinion.

A warning

Imagine yourself there among the crowds. You have heard this clever bandying of words. Now you watch as Jesus turns to the crowds around him in the Temple and starts to tell you all a story – an allegory. Remember, you have no knowledge of Jesus' death yet, only a frightening sense that something awful or wonderful will happen soon. Read the story Jesus tells in Mark 12 : 1–11.

Research and questions

1. If you were a Jew you would know that a vineyard stood for the Jewish nation.
   Who was the owner of the vineyard?
   Who were: (*a*) the tenants? (*b*) the servants sent to collect the fruit (the rent)? (*c*) the son whom they killed and threw out?
2. When was this prophecy fulfilled?
3. Read and compare Isaiah 5 : 1–7. Isaiah's prophecy was fulfilled 600 years earlier. What happened to the Jews then?
4. The words in Mark 12 : 10–11 come from the Jewish book of songs and poems, the book of Psalms. Find them in Psalm 118 and state in which verses they occur.
5. Who would you understand to be the 'stone', and who the 'builders'?
6. Are you surprised at the result of this parable? See Mark 12 : 12. Who do you think 'they' are?
   Read Luke 20 : 19–20 and Matt. 21 : 45–46 to see if you are right. You need both these references.
7. What reasons can you think of which Jesus might have had for telling this story at this point?

C Paying the Roman taxes

Mark 12 : 13–17. Now we come to the second question Jesus was asked.

Research and questions

1. What was the question, and who asked it?
2. Why was it a normal subject for argument between the two parties who asked the question?
3. How did they try to get round him by flattery? Was it genuine?
4. Which words of Jesus show that he saw through their flatteries?

5. The silver piece was a Roman coin. The Romans had put these coins into circulation so that the Jews could pay their taxes in Roman money. Jewish money was useless to the Romans in other parts of their empire.

Think out (*a*) if Jesus had said a direct 'Yes, you should pay these taxes', in answer to the question, who would have been angry, and why? (*b*) if he had said 'No', of what could he have been accused, and by whom punished?

6. Why were the crowds astonished at the answer he gave?

7. Apart from avoiding trouble, what did he teach by his answer?
   To help you think this out, read and discuss these notes:
   (*a*) Think about taxes – they are not really *gifts* to the government. They are payment for services rendered, e.g. your education, defence for your country, good roads for your travel, proper government for the country, etc. Is this true? Think of some of the services the Romans were rendering.
   (*b*) Now think of your money, your possessions, your very life? Did you create them for yourself? You and your parents may have earned your money. People made your possessions and you bought them or were given them as a gift. You yourself are here because of the union of your parents.

   Did man create life in the first place, and the conditions to make life possible all down the ages? If not, to what greater power do we owe these gifts? Discuss this.

   What would be the answer of Jesus and the Jews to this question?

NOTE: The word 'Render' can be translated as 'Give back' or 'Pay . . . what is due'. (*N.E.B.*)

D A question about resurrection

Mark 12 : 18–27

Research and questions

1. What was the third question? By whom was it asked?
2. What did the Sadducees think about the idea of resurrection?
3. Did they genuinely want to know the answer, or just to make Jesus look ridiculous and discredit him?
4. How did his reply, in which he quoted from Exodus 3 : 6, show up their ignorance? What did he say were the two reasons for their error? Mark 12 : 24.

E A genuine question?

Research and questions

1. Read Mark 12 : 28–34. One scribe (lawyer, *N.E.B.*) (perhaps of the first group of questioners of Mark 11 : 27) admired Jesus' replies. What was his own question? Remember the scribes were the guardians of the Law, the experts in its details.
2. After Jesus had answered, what were the first three words the scribe said? (*N.E.B.*, first four words in *R.S.V.*)
3. To understand why the scribe admired Jesus' reply to his own question even more, we need to realise that it came from two widely separated parts of the Jewish Law. Jesus had picked them out, showing that he, too, had a thorough knowledge of the Law.

   Find these two references and state which part of Jesus' answer came from each reference: Deut. 6 : 4–5 and Lev. 19 : 18.
4. What did Jesus say which showed he knew that the scribe's reply was genuine?
5. What was the result of all the trickery the Jewish leaders had tried on him that day? Mark 12 : 34. Would you say that their efforts had met with success or failure?
6. Jesus had spent a hard day dealing with the evil intrigues of the rival parties of the Jewish leaders who should all, by their professions, have been working with him for God. It led him to warn the people against judging by the outward signs of importance and goodness. Mark 12 : 38–40. What did the Jewish leaders love? What did they do?
7. To see the real love of God in someone just before he left the Temple must have been a great relief to him. What did he see? Mark 12 : 41–44. Discuss the comment Jesus made.

3 The Suffering Servant

A Does God suffer?

Matthew writes that during the last week in Jerusalem Jesus told a number of parables. One of them shows an aspect of God which makes Christianity unique among world religions. Read Matt. 25 : 31–46.

Research and questions

1. What is your conception of God? Do you think of him as:
   (a) apart in some heavenly place, too far removed to be interested in the petty affairs of ordinary people?
   (b) apart in some heavenly place, looking down in sorrow at the sufferings of men – sometimes putting out a 'long arm' to help them?
   (c) far greater than we can understand, yet closely identified with each one of us, sharing our joys and suffering?
2. Which of these conceptions do you find in the following part of the parable we have just read:

   I was hungry and you gave me food, I was thirsty and you gave me drink, I was a stranger and you welcomed me, I was naked and you clothed me, I was sick and you visited me, I was in prison and you came to me . . . as you did it to one of the least of these my brethren, you did it to me?

3. What have Jesus' life and his teaching in this parable shown us about God's assessment of the value of every human being?
   For private thought: Think of someone whom you do not consider important, or whose suffering you disregard. What difference does Christ's picture presented in this parable make to your own attitude?
4. Give the names of two Christians who through medicine have done an outstanding work to relieve suffering, and say what their achievements were.
5. Where is there suffering in the world today? What are Christians doing about it?
6. The problem of suffering has exercised people's minds down the ages. It is a big subject. Many who have suffered have been conscious of Christ's companionship and felt that what he went through as man meant that he could understand. Here are two examples:

EXAMPLE I: ST FRANCIS OF ASSISI
During his stay in the East, Francis contracted trachoma, an eye disease.

Both his eyes were painfully inflamed and swollen. The light of day – which he had loved so much because in it he saw men and trees and flowers and birds and all the other things of beauty in God's creation – lost its splendour and vanished at times.

Francis accepted all this without a trace of bitterness. His love and his trust in God remained unshaken. . . . For all this grief came from the same Creator that had favoured him for so long with an abundance of joy and happiness – God who had not seen fit to save His only-begotten Son from the bitterest grief, the most painful sorrow; from treason and death, since from that suffering came the rescue of God's loved human creatures from worse ills. Death and martyrdom were the beginning of the miracle of resurrection. How small, how pitifully small, was Francis's grief compared with the passion of Christ.

For Francis there was only one approach to all things. All his relationships meant love. It was love that taught him to accept pain. And he did not endure it; he embraced it with brotherly tenderness. 'Oh, Lord!' he prayed, 'grant me the joy of enduring your grief.' It was then that he wrote his poem of thanksgiving to God for the splendour of his creation.

Adapted from *Saints that Moved the World*, René Fülop-Miller (Hutchinson)

EXAMPLE 2: A NORWEGIAN IMPRISONED BY THE GESTAPO

Leif Hovelsen had seen his friends taken away to a concentration camp. He himself had been beaten. Now the Gestapo told him he would be executed.

'Execution! For what? Everything in me shouted to be let live. I could not grasp that this might be the end . . . I knew that prayer was my one hope. "Whatever be your will, God", I said, "let that come to pass. But if I may live and even be free once again, I give you the whole of my life for you to use as you will."

'In the days that followed I began to think about Christ. Up to then I felt I did not understand him. But now, having been betrayed and beaten and standing face to face with death, all he had gone through became real to me. What he had suffered was far far more than what was happening to me. It was like Jesus walking by my side and saying to me, "Don't be afraid. I have done all this for you. I am conqueror."

'These were the richest days I have ever lived through.'

From *Out of the Evil Night*, Leif Hovelsen (Blandford), also in *Readings for the Senior Assembly*, D. M. Prescott (Blandford).

Question: What was the effect of the prayer struggle in each story?

SOME SUGGESTED BOOKS FOR QUESTION NO. 4

Joseph Lister, F. F. Cartwright (Weidenfeld & Nicolson).
The Story of a Labrador Doctor, Wilfred Grenfell (Hodder & Stoughton).
Dr Schweitzer of Lambaréné, N. Cousins (A. & C. Black).
No doubt you will find others in the library.

B Why did Judas betray Jesus?

We are told very little about what happened on the Wednesday of Easter week. But what we are told is crucial. On that day Judas began to carry out his plot to betray Jesus. Read Matt. 26 : 6–16.

Research and questions

1. What event triggered off Judas' betrayal? Why were the disciples critical?
2. What was Jesus' reply to the disciples? What did it mean?
3. Imagine the joy of the chief priests at getting the co-operation of one of Jesus' followers! Having used his help, how did they treat him when he went back to them full of remorse? (Matt. 27 : 4.)
4. People have discussed for centuries why Judas betrayed Jesus.
   (*a*) Some quote Matt. 26 : 15 and back it up with John 12 : 6 and 13 : 29 to show that the reason was a defect in Judas's character. What defect?
   (*b*) Others think that Judas became impatient and wanted to force Jesus to show himself as the Messiah-King – that he thought Jesus would do so once he was arrested. He could not believe that Jesus would really let himself be killed. To back up this point of view they quote what Judas did when he found that Jesus was condemned. What was that? Matt. 27 : 3–5.
   (*c*) Another view is that Judas went over to the other side when he saw that Jesus appeared to be losing to his enemies.
   You may like to discuss all these possibilities.

C The farewell supper

If you have a party for your friends I expect you plan it and buy what is needed. Perhaps other friends help?

To the disciples the meal they prepared on Thursday was part of the normal Passover celebrations. To Jesus it was to be far more. He seems to have taken much trouble over where it was to be held, preparing for it in secrecy.

Read of these preparations in Mark 14 : 12–16, or Luke 22 : 7–13.

Luke tells us it was Peter and John whom Jesus sent to prepare the meal.

What gives the sense of secret plans in this reading? A man was

rarely seen carrying a water-pot (it was a woman's job), so he would be easy to spot. Note where the disciples were to be before they spoke. Why was this, do you think?

Have you ever thought why it should be that a party centres round a meal – a gift of food? This has been so since earliest man shared his meals with·neighbours. It is a sign of friendship. Heaven was often thought of as a Great Feast with God.

In primitive days men felt that their gods should be fed. The way to their favour lay in offering them a meal. It sealed a bond of unity between man and god.

The Jews, in Old Testament days, used to offer to God the best part of their animal sacrifice, the fat, by burning it on the altar. They would eat the rest themselves, so sharing the meal. But they would not eat the blood. That was God's: it was the life of the sacrificed creature. They poured it on to, or at the foot of, the altar.

Research and questions

1. Read Exodus 24 : 1–8 and see how Moses at Sinai sealed the Covenant between God and the Israelites in blood; half was thrown against the altar then, after they had promised to keep their side of the bargain, he sprinkled the other half over them.

   Now read of what took place at the Last Supper in Matt. 26 : 20–29; Mark 14 : 18–25.

   In days gone by it was the best animal of the flock which was sacrificed. Here was Jesus pointing a new way: he was not offering his best possession, but himself, to unite men with God. His body in place of the meat (bread), his blood in place of the animal's blood. This sacrifice was made so that men could start a new life with God.

2. Do you think the twelve (or eleven if Judas had left by then, as John seems to indicate) understood what Jesus was doing? If not then, when do you think they would understand?

3. Why do you think Jesus was acting this sacrifice in this symbolic way with bread and wine before he actually gave himself in sacrifice on the Cross?

4. When do Christians celebrate this Last Supper now? What is this ceremony called? – It has a number of names.

5. What does the word Communion mean? What do you think the Lord's Supper means to sincere Christians?

6. It was mentioned in an earlier question that Judas Iscariot left early. Where had he gone? What did Jesus say about him before he left?

7. John gives a much fuller account of what Jesus said and did at this meal. John 13 : 3 (R.S.V.) reads: 'Jesus, knowing that the Father had given all things into his hands, and that he had come from God and was going to God, rose from supper. . . .' Read on to verse 11. What did he do then? Read what he said afterwards. John 13 : 12–17.

Further work

Read and study with your teacher the other parts of what Jesus said at the Last Supper, as told in John's gospel.

D Waiting for the test – Gethsemane

What do you do just before a test – in schoolwork, sport or in any other situation? Do you say, 'I can take it!' and have a rest, or do you worry? Compare how Jesus spent the time before his great test with the way the disciples spent it. Read Mark 14 : 26–42.

Research and questions

1. 'After singing the Passover Hymn, they went out . . .' (N.E.B.) Find these words in Mark 14 and read of the events on the way to the Garden of Gethsemane. What was Peter's reply to Jesus' warning about their desertion?
2. Have you ever felt sure you would not fail and yet done so? As you know, Peter found later that his own strength was not sufficient. What did he need?
3. Read the next verses, 32–42. What did Jesus tell Peter, James and John to do? What did he add to this when he came back and found them sleeping? Do you think it would have helped them to meet the test if they had done this?
4. How do you think Jesus felt when he found his friends asleep?
5. Copy out Jesus' prayer and underline the words which show Jesus' complete trust in his Father. Do you think his prayer would have helped him? If so, in what way?
6. Arrested! Write an account of the arrest bringing in all the details you can learn from the descriptions in all four gospels: Matt. 26 : 47–56, Mark 14 : 43–52, Luke 22 : 47–53 and John 18 : 2–12.

NOTE: The 'young man' is only mentioned in Mark's gospel. This makes it apparent that John Mark was the young man. Why was he there clad in only a sheet? To help you think about this, remember that the Last Supper had probably been held in John Mark's mother's upper room.

4   Jesus Christ Pays the Price

A   Silent!

Jesus was led off to the house of the high priest, in the depths of the night, and underwent a trial, illegal though it was.

The accusations against him were hard to find and did not agree when they were found. They were all to do with points in the Jewish religion, and as such would hold no weight with the Roman authorities. If Jesus was to die, the Romans had to give their consent. The Jews condemned him and then had to wait until morning to find a way to accuse him legally before the Romans.

Hurriedly at dawn another trial was held and the accusations twisted to make Jesus appear a traitor to Rome. He was to be accused of inciting the crowds to rebellion and setting himself up as a new King of the Jews. This would be counted as treason by the Romans and worthy of death.

With this, the priests marched him off to the house of the Roman governor, who was in Jerusalem at this time of the Passover festival in case of trouble. He usually resided in Caesarea.

Research and questions

1. When you are falsely accused do you:
   (*a*) keep quiet;
   (*b*) speak out, defending yourself;
   (*c*) say only those things which are for the future good of your accusers – even if it leads you into further trouble?
2. Which of these did Jesus do? Read Matt. 26 : 57–68.
3. What did Jesus actually say, and what effect did it have on his accusers?
4. Jesus was kept under guard during the rest of the night. How was he treated by the guards? *See also* Luke 22 : 63–65.

B   Helpless!

We are told that Peter followed Jesus to the trial held that night in the high priest's house. John's gospel (chapter 18) gives an explanation of how he gained admittance to the courtyard. Remember how Peter had said he would die with Jesus rather than disown him. Can you imagine what his feelings were now?

Research and questions

1. Read the account in Matt. 26 : 69–75. Try to imagine all Peter felt throughout this episode and write your own account.
2. There is a saying, 'Man's extremity . . .' Complete the sentence.
   To understand this saying let us consider further what happened to Peter.
   (*a*) Until this point Peter had always felt sure of himself, that he would be successful, that he knew best. How did he show this in the events described in Luke 5 : 4–11 and Matt. 16 : 21–23?
   (*b*) Now in a devastating way Peter learnt that his own wisdom was not enough. He had failed when he thought he was strong. How had he failed?
   (*c*) He had to learn to trust God, not himself. God could help him to do much more than he would ever dream of doing in his own strength. Describe shortly one of these occasions from Acts 2, 3, 4 or 10.
   (*d*) Explain now 'Man's extremity is God's opportunity'.
   (*e*) From all this, do you think it is sometimes a good thing to fail?

C Mob rule ?

The next run of events gives an example of how a few determined men can overrule a powerful governor and use a mob to gain their own ends. From now until the end of these studies it is suggested that you might work in groups of four, looking up specific gospels and reading aloud to the others and discussing answers together (except where asked to do otherwise).

Research and questions

1. Read of all that happened on Good Friday morning, well before 9 a.m.! Luke 23 : 1–25, Matt. 27 : 1–2 and 11–26 (Mark's account is much the same). Finally read John 18 : 28 to 19 : 16.
2. What differences do you notice between Matthew's and Luke's accounts?
3. Which of the three versions helps you to picture it most vividly?

4. Do you understand why John tells how the priests stayed outside the Roman governor's house instead of going in? If not, find out. Then explain why it was.
5. What was the only question Jesus answered in Matthew's and Luke's accounts? What effect did Jesus' lack of self-defence have on Pilate?
6. Write out as a play the conversation of Jesus with Pilate, as given in John's account:

    Pilate – Are you . . .

    Jesus – Is it . . . etc.

    If possible use the *New English Bible*.
7. What happened to make Pilate, usually utterly ruthless, afraid to have Jesus put to death (to be found only in Matthew's gospel)?
8. The priests made Pilate feel afraid of what would happen if he did *not* have Jesus put to death. Pilate had great power under Caesar. Yet he could be deprived of this power if he lost Caesar's favour, for he would lose his job. Historians tell us that he had already made mistakes in dealing with the Jewish rebelliousness, which had brought criticism from Rome.

    How did the priests use the mob (the crowds now gathered with them outside the governor's residence) to make Pilate afraid not to condemn Jesus, even though he seemed innocent?
9. Can you see that now Pilate was 'between the devil and the deep blue sea'? He chose to do what he knew was wrong. How did he try to get rid of the blame? Why did he want to get rid of it? – He wasn't usually so worried.
10. If you had been a Jew in that crowd outside Pilate's house, what do you think you would have done? Would you have been a careless onlooker? Would you have cared, but kept quiet through fear? Would you have been persuaded to join in and call out: 'Crucify him'? Each of these types of people helped to kill Jesus. Explain how. Notice that we do not hear of anyone calling for Jesus' release. Can you suggest why?

D It is accomplished!

The best introduction to this section is for Mark's account of the crucifixion to be read aloud by a good reader who has prepared it beforehand. It is in Mark 15 : 16–39. Afterwards the class should spend a few moments quietly and write down any thoughts arising from the reading.

Research and questions

1. Describe the mockery of the soldiers before the procession to Golgotha.

2. Cyrene is in North Africa. Simon may have been an African slave or servant – or a Jew living in that part of the world. What does Mark say about his family? Rufus is mentioned as a good Christian in Rome at one point in Paul's letter to the Romans (Romans 16 : 13). Probably these sons were well known to some who would be reading Mark's gospel.

3. Luke was always interested in the part women played. What did he notice about them in Luke 23 : 27? What did Jesus mean and predict in his reply? Luke 23 : 28–31. Does it not seem amazing that after all he had been through, and was still undergoing, that he could think for them in this way?

4. The 'third hour' was 9 a.m. You can work out from this the other times mentioned. At what time was Jesus crucified? When did he die? When did it become dark? All this information can be found in Mark.

5. What does John's gospel tell us about the title on Jesus' cross? John 19 : 17–22.

6. Still in John's gospel, the next verses 23–24, what does it say the soldiers were doing as Jesus hung on the cross? (Lloyd Douglas's book *The Robe* [Peter Davies] gives a vivid account of this.)

7. In their mocking, which of Jesus' three temptations in the wilderness were the passers-by putting to Jesus again? Which verses in Mark's account give this?

8. Jesus spoke a number of times from the cross, perhaps more than we are told. Here is a summary taken from all four gospels. Find and give the reference in each case and answer the questions:
   (*a*) 'Father forgive them; they do not know what they are doing.' Who were 'they' in this quotation? What part of his own teaching was Jesus living out in making this prayer?
   (*b*) 'I tell you this: today you shall be with me in Paradise.' To whom was Jesus saying this?
   (*c*) 'Mother, there is your son' . . . 'There is your mother.' Who were 'mother' and 'son'? Can you care for people around you like this when you are in great pain?
   (*d*) 'I thirst.' What was offered to him then?
   (*e*) 'My God, my God, why hast thou forsaken me?'
       Of which Psalm is this the first line? Find two other parts of this Psalm which remind us of the crucifixion of Jesus.

(*f*) 'It is accomplished.' What was accomplished?

(*g*) 'Father, into thy hands I commit my spirit.' What happened then?

9. Who said 'Truly this man was a son of God'? (*N.E.B.* footnote to 1970 edition gives 'the Son of God'). Was this a surprising remark from this man? If so, why?

10. Which women were watching?

E Easter Saturday

This is a day often passed over without much thought given to it. We will spend a little time thinking about it.

Can you imagine the feelings of the disciples on that Sabbath Saturday? Remember, they had never really understood that Jesus would go so far as to die. This meant of course that they had not thought ahead to any 'rising from the dead'. His presence was no longer with them to reassure them. Was that the end? Had it all been just a wonderful dream? They had given up everything for that dream. Were they to go back to their old lives and pick up the threads again? What were they to do? They must have felt utterly lost.

Think of Peter's feelings. The last Jesus had seen of him was at his denial. What was John doing? He would have Jesus' mother to care about, and she would surely be in great need. What of the other disciples? We have not heard of them since they all forsook Jesus and fled.

We cannot answer these questions. There is no record. All we can do is to guess at the sorrow and emptiness of that Sabbath day – except of course to the Jewish leaders and the unthinking public. They too would be talking about the events of Good Friday.

Research and questions

1. What is the evidence that everyone in Jerusalem was discussing Jesus' crucifixion on Easter Saturday? Luke 24 : 18.

2. What do you think the women would be doing after the Sabbath ended at 6 p.m. on that day? Remember they had not had time to finish what they were doing when the Sabbath day began at 6 p.m. on the Friday. Nor could they continue after 6 p.m. on Saturday as it would be too dark to see in the tomb.

3. One event of the Saturday is recorded – only one. Find out what it was from Matt. 27 : 62–66.

5 Triumph! God is Indestructible

Then came that amazing 'first day of the week', the first Easter Day. Is the Resurrection true? Let us do some detective work. Try to forget all you have learned about it in the past and investigate every point for yourself before you make up your mind.

A Resurrection

Research and questions

1. Read Matt. 28 : 1, Mark 16 : 1–2, Luke 24 : 1, John 20 : 1.
   (*a*) What day of the week was it?
   (*b*) At what time of day was the tomb found empty?
2. The same verses plus Luke 24 : 10 will help you with the next questions.
   (*a*) Do all the gospels agree on who discovered the empty tomb first?
   (*b*) You will have discovered that John's gospel only mentions one woman. Read what she 'cried' to Peter in verse 2 in that chapter. Which word there shows that others were involved?
   (*c*) List the names of those who were there, from all the gospel accounts.
3. Read Luke 23 : 55–24 : 1, Mark 15 : 47–6 : 1, Matt. 28 : 1.
   (*a*) What were the women coming to do? (John gives no reason.)
   (*b*) Read on a little. Which gospel mentions a problem the women were discussing as they approached the tomb? What was it?
   (*c*) Look back at the accounts of Jesus's burial to see which gospels mention this obstacle: Matt. 27 : 57–61, Mark 15 : 42–47, Luke 23 : 50–54, John 19 : 38–42.
   (*d*) Do you think it was possible for Joseph of Arimathaea to accomplish all this on his own? Which gospel tells us he had someone to help him? Who was he?
   (*e*) Do the gospels all agree on the reason why the problem was unfounded? State what each affirms.
   (*f*) Did the women ever accomplish what they set out to do [as in (*a*)]? Why or why not?
4. Read Matt. 28 : 1–8, Mark 16 : 1–8, Luke 24 : 1–11, John 20 : 1–18.
   Mention some of the discrepancies between the accounts of what was seen and heard at the tomb that morning.
5. (*a*) Get four of your number to describe something to which they were all witnesses some time ago. Notice the details of difference.

(*b*) If the disciples had got together to deceive by pretending Jesus had risen from the dead, do you think their accounts would have differed as they do?

(*c*) What do you deduce from your answers to these two points and from all your investigations about the truth or otherwise of the Resurrection?

FURTHER READING

Who Moved the Stone? Frank Morison (Faber).

B Jesus' Resurrection appearances

For forty days after this Jesus made a number of appearances to his followers, some noted by each of the gospel writers.

Here we will only take two such occasions. The first is in John 21 : 15–19. Earlier in the chapter we are told that five disciples were back at their old occupation of fishing, up in the north on the Lake of Tiberias. Find it on the map (p. 91). After breakfasting with them, Jesus had a conversation with Peter alone.

The second occasion was also in the north. The meeting-place with Jesus was at a mountain in Galilee, apparently prearranged with the disciples. (Matt. 28 : 16–20.)

Research and questions (may be taken orally)

1. Why do you think Jesus asked Peter three times if he loved him?
2. Thinking of what Peter had done since we last heard about him, and all he must have been thinking and feeling since then, what do you think this encounter meant to him?
3. What was Jesus' message to his disciples on the second occasion?
4. Do you think the words 'make disciples of all nations' was a new idea to them? If so, in what ways? And in what other ways may it not have been quite so new?
5. What was Jesus' final promise to them?

Further work

Working in your groups of four, make a book of the Resurrection appearances, using all four gospels, each group writing of a different event. Complete each account with a description of the Ascension as narrated by Luke in Acts 1. Give it a title and arrange the book as your group thinks best.

Add illustrations and poems you find or make up yourself on the subject. Afterwards the books can be exchanged between groups for reading and comparison of their different approaches.

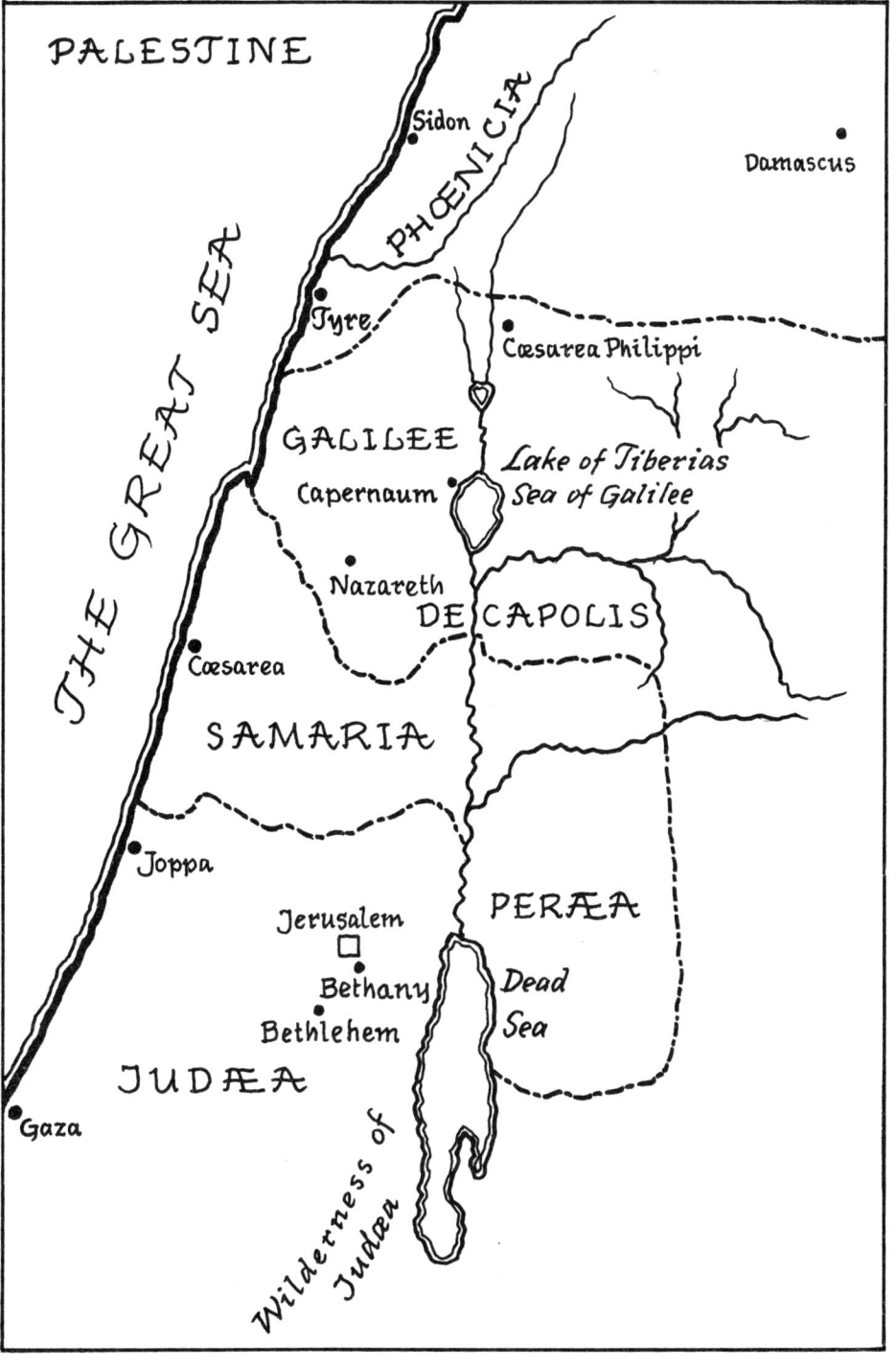

Section VI

THE NEW SOCIETY SPREADS

The assignments in this section will require a considerable amount of time and research.

1 The Cross of Christ will Transform the World

A great Christian leader of the twentieth century has spoken of 'The greatest revolution of all time whereby the Cross of Christ will transform the world.'

We all recognise the need for change in the world, but we may not understand how the Cross of Christ could effect this transformation. Historians have agreed that the Cross did bring about a world transformation in the first centuries after Christ. In considering how that took place we may see possibilities for today's world.

At the beginning of the first Whitsun there were only a few hundred men and women believers in Jerusalem. By the end of the day there were about three thousand more (Acts 2 : 41). Today there are millions across the world. The lives, cultures and traditions of many nations have been deeply affected. How did the first few ordinary Christians find the faith and the power and the way to affect the world so radically?

To answer this, we first need to think of the kind of people we are. Human nature is the same in every century. Then we need to see what Christ's life, death and resurrection meant (and still mean) to his followers.

Do you ever feel that however much you try to live right you fail? You seem to have to compromise – to tell little white lies, or bigger ones; to be angry or unkind; to choose one of several courses, all wrong. You feel guilty, but there seems no other way to live. People have always felt like this. Some decide to live as if nothing matters. Look at the selfishness there has always been in the world, and the unhappiness it brings.

Yet when Jesus came he lived as men ought to live, never allowing outside pressure to make him deviate from accepting God's will in his heart and so in his actions. He suffered and died. If that had been all, men would have said, 'There you are, that's what happens if you do God's will completely. There is no hope.'

Soon after his death his followers began to make a startling assertion. They had seen Jesus again. He had risen from the dead to bring men new life. They now understood that in spite of all men's failures and wickedness he had died to put them right with God; and that he was still alive and with them. Men had but to repent, to give up their lives of compromise and dare to let God take control, and they could have this new inward, triumphant life – eternal life, beginning on earth and continuing after death. Jesus Christ had said he would always be with them, and that the Holy Spirit would give them power to take his message to the whole world. A new era had begun.

The faith and the power

The new age begins in men's hearts. Jesus never promised a life of ease and comfort. He did promise that those who follow him shall find purpose and power to live triumphantly and effectively. That this is so, Christians down the ages have proved by their own experiences. Let us see what it meant to two of the men first responsible for taking Christianity out to the world.

Research and questions

1. PETER (*a*) What change did Jesus' death and resurrection bring to Peter. (Acts 2 : 14.)?
   (*b*) Contrast Peter disowning Jesus in the high priest's courtyard with Peter as we see him in Acts 3 and 4. What is the difference? What do you think caused it?
   (*c*) What power had Peter learnt to rely on in place of his earlier self-sufficiency? Look up the following references to check your answer: Acts 2 : 4, 4 : 8, 10 : 44–48, 11 : 15–17.
2. PAUL We read earlier (p. 26) how, as Saul, he had persecuted the Christians, and led the violence against them. Find out all you can about him up to this time, from Acts 7 : 58 and 9 : 1–30: also from books such as *A Rushing Mighty Wind* by Mary Wilson and *The Living Faith*, Book 3, by T. G. Platten.
   (*a*) What was Saul's aim before the events on the road to Damascus?
   (*b*) What was his aim afterwards?
   (*c*) Read Paul's explanation of the way he saw the work of Jesus in one of his letters, 2 Cor. 5 : 14–17 – R.S.V.
      (i) Why did Christ die? (verse 15).
      (ii) What should our new purpose be? (verse 15).
      (iii) How would this change of motives make us 'a new creation'? (verse 17). What would be shaping our lives?

(*d*) Read how Saul after his isolated years in Tarsus came to join the growing body of Christians in Antioch in Syria. It was from here he set out later to spread the news of Christ across the world. Acts 11 : 19–26. Most of the Christians in Antioch were Gentiles. Discuss why Barnabas may have felt Saul was needed there.

B The Way

We read in Acts 12 : 24 that 'the word of God grew and multiplied' and in Acts 11 : 20–21 how the Christians who fled after the stoning of Stephen spread the gospel and many more became Christians. All the events recorded in Acts led to further outreach.

One of history's most dramatic turning-points is vividly portrayed for us in Acts 13 : 1–14. It began in Syrian Antioch, the great Mediterranean harbour city where the trade-routes of three continents blended, and where the followers of Jesus were first called Christians. Verse 1 lists the leading Christians there. Whose name comes first? Whose last? In verse 2 two of these are selected for a journey. Who is no. 1? Who no. 2?

Barnabas, meaning 'Consoler', was the nickname for a big, happy Jew of Cyprus named Joseph. He owned lands, sold them and gave the apostles the proceeds (Acts 4 : 36). His sister provided the Upper Room to which Peter ran when freed from prison (Acts 12), probably also that used for the Last Supper. Here his nephew John Mark lived. Mark had gone with Barnabas to Antioch and now went with Barnabas and Saul as their attendant, to Cyprus, his ancestral home.

Saul, which means 'wanted', was the Hebrew name of the little learned Jew who had persecuted the Christians until he was blinded by the sight of Jesus on the Damascus Road. His father was a Roman citizen. Brought by Barnabas from his isolation in Tarsus in Asia Minor to help in Antioch, he now found himself about to set out for Cyprus.

They landed on the east coast at Salamis, now Famagusta, where you can still walk on the actual pavement of the shopping-centre (forum) they trod. They went from synagogue to synagogue along the south coast until they reached lovely Paphos (Limassol today) basking in the sun on the seashore under 6,000 ft. Mt Troödos. Here they were called into the audience hall of the Roman Proconsul Sergius Paulus.

We might imagine the scene. Up a flight of three or four broad shallow steps sits the governor on his chair of office in the cool shady hall with a fountain splashing into its central pool. Behind the chair stands his adviser whose name Elymas is in Hebrew 'Aleem' and in Persian 'Magus' meaning 'Wise Man'. (You recall the three Wise Men from the East were 'Magi'). This Magus had the governor's ear. Sergius Paulus' service in the East had clearly opened his mind to other faiths than Rome's idolatry. He was genuinely seeking a higher way of life for himself and Rome. Elymas naturally did not want to lose his influence over the governor.

Before him on the lower level stand three Jews. Barnabas, until then the leader, may have spoken first. Elymas interrupts all the time, trying to turn the governor against all that is being said. He has the advantage over Barnabas of being learned and well travelled. Saul cannot stand it. Here is God giving them the chance to move out of narrow Jewish circles to influence the very leaders of the Roman Empire itself, and they are not getting anywhere. The governor's second name is Paul: it burns in on Saul that his own second name is Paul likewise, and that 'Paul' carries with it the full significance of his Roman citizenship. He can use this name to win the Romans' confidence. God is pointing out to them His Straight Way to win the world and Elymas is blinding the governor to it, and pushing them all off the Lord's Way. A surge of conviction makes him stride out into the lead and into his full Roman heritage.

Verse 9 puts it in a few words: 'Then Saul, who is Paul, filled with the Spirit, said . . .' He is never called Saul again in the New Testament. From now on he is Paul. He gave Elymas the same gift of physical blindness as he himself had been given by God in Damascus . . . to be blind for a season in which to see the error of his ways . . . and he won the governor to understand the Way.

But in his surge of passion another way had dawned on his mind – the straight ways of the Lord, and also the Royal Road of the Persian emperors from Susa to Europe, now extended by the Romans to Rome. He saw it as the straight way for the gospel to reach Rome and so to all the world. He must make for that road. Its nearest spot to Paphos lay in Pisidia in Asia Minor at a town also called Antioch like its Syrian namesake. He set out to reach it and for the rest of his life never left the highway of the empire.

In verse 13 who is leader now? and what has happened to the others?

Research and questions follow the map on page 98.

Research and questions

1. Find out with the help of your teacher, what Paul's vision of the Way led to:

    (*a*) setting Asia Minor in a ferment;

    (*b*) having to stand up to the Jews who wanted everyone to conform to outward Jewish observances before they could become Christians. (Notice how Paul made it clear that it was inward and moral change not outward conformity which marked out a follower of Christ – Acts 15);

    (*c*) carrying the good news to Europe and on to the empire centre, Rome;

    (*d*) writing letters to the new Christians, to encourage and help them over their difficulties and failings;

    (*e*) facing dangers and opposition of every kind with great courage.

    From Acts 13 onwards and the books mentioned under Paul in the last section you will find help in your researches.

2. Find out where it is thought that other apostles took the Christian message. See *A Rushing Mighty Wind*, Mary Wilson, pp. 95 and 114.

3. *God's Hand in History* is the title of Mary Wilson's series. Write an essay showing how God's 'Hand' can be traced through Paul's life and work.

2 Decisions that Affect Nations

From these early beginnings, right through the centuries, men and women in many lands have given everything to bring about this transformation. They made the decision to do God's will and not their own for the rest of their lives; and entrusted themselves to God, not knowing where he would lead them.

For the Christians, 'taking up the cross' means making this decision and continuing to make it in all the big and little affairs of life. Opposition, danger, death itself have never been able to stamp out Christianity.

A In past centuries

Research and questions

1. Read about one of the following early Christians who suffered persecution and write a short account: Polycarp, Perpetua, Felicity, St Alban. Find out and say what their constancy led to for other people.
2. Study the lives and influence on education and culture of two of the founders of monasteries and colleges. Examples: Gregory of Armenia, Benedict, Alcuin, Anselm, Bernard of Clairvaux.
3. Find out about Patrick's work in Druid Ireland and discover from this how a country became Christian through the work of a dedicated man. Note how at the end he was able to work out with the High King new civil laws more in keeping with the new Christian regime. Find out what some of these changes were. What decision did Patrick have to make before he could take on this work? What smaller but important decisions do you imagine he had to make day after day during the years of his work there?
4. Discover what you can about the origins of some Christian features of British life today. For instance, how and when was it first established in Britain that kings and queens should be anointed and crowned at a church service, thus dedicating their reign to God? Why has Parliament from its beginning opened its proceedings with prayer?

The Imperial State Crown. This was worn by Her Majesty Queen Elizabeth II at her coronation on 2nd June 1953.

5. Keir Hardie was the first Labour MP in the House of Commons. He wrote in his diary of his becoming a Christian at the age of twenty-three and said that from that time: 'Christianity became the chief inspiration and driving power of my life.' What effect did his being a Christian have on his fight for the rights of the working class? *If possible,* quote two key phrases he used (*See Brave Men Choose,* G. D. Lean, pp. 168, 171, 179, 182).

Some recommended books for 1–3

A Rushing Mighty Wind, Mary Wilson (Blandford).
Builders and Destroyers, Mary Wilson (Blandford).
Founders of Europe I and II, Martha Scott-Moncrieff (Blandford).
The Steadfast Man, Paul Gallico (Michael Joseph).

References for No. 4

Encyclopaedia Britannica (Vol. 6, Coronation) (Wm. Benton).
An Encyclopaedia of Parliament, Norman Wilding and Philip Laundy (Cassell), p. 556.
The British Constitution, J. Harvey and L. Bather (Macmillan).

B In our day

Research and questions

1. Try to find out about anyone living today who has taken a costly decision to do God's work in the world. What was the decision and what is the result?
2. Why do you think people want to give their lives to the direction of God? What enables them to pay the price with faith and hope? Read Paul's answer to this in Rom. 8 : 35–39.
3. In what ways do you think the lives and relationships of people and nations could change today if enough men and women let God control their lives?
4. Write out a few practical ways in which you and your classmates could set out to make the class, the school, the district, models of the sort of world of brotherhood, purity and justice which Jesus taught.

Section VII

JESUS IN THE WORLD OF
TODAY AND TOMORROW

The New Society in Practice

How could Jesus affect the society of today – and tomorrow?

The following questions need much thought and research. For some of them you may be able to work in groups and then exchange findings with other groups.

It is important that you do not merely state opinions, but fully support your arguments with quotations and examples from Jesus' life and teaching, and from other appropriate sources. For some of the questions you may like to start scrap-books using newspapers and getting statistics, etc., and you will need to find relevant books, for which the teacher or librarian will be able to give assistance. For some, you can use work done on earlier assignments.

Research and questions

1. How does society value people? Answer this through the following questions:
   (a) In a crowd, some people are left out and neglected. If you are one of these, how do you feel? Even if you are not, do you like being one of a number? Give reasons.
   (b) When society as a whole thinks of the problem of old people, what solutions are put forward? When the old person is someone you love, do you feel differently about him/her? If so, in what way?
   (c) What evidences are there in house-building of people being treated as though they were all alike? What makes it difficult to do otherwise? What problems does this mass treatment bring to some of the people and children who live in these dwellings? How could their needs be better catered for?
   (d) Can we expect governments to provide for everybody's needs all the time? How far do you think governments will ever be able to do this while the people in the nations are selfish?
2. Jesus Christ has the responsibility for bringing the whole of mankind to God. How does he regard the individual? Give examples

from his life and teaching to illustrate your answer. Does a Christian need to feel alone? Give reasons for your reply.

3. General Booth lived in a time of great poverty in the late nineteenth century. His care for any individual in need was inspired by his love of Christ, and he went to great lengths to relieve suffering. Through the Salvation Army, which he founded, employment, hostels and food were provided in many countries. But he felt certain that only through God could a complete answer come, and in his book *Darkest England – and the Way Out* he wrote:

> 'My only hope for the permanent deliverance of mankind from misery is the . . . remaking of the individual by the power of the Holy Ghost through Jesus Christ.'

How far could change in people bring about a change in present-day society?

4. Today men and women of differing faiths, cultures and traditions are living together in a multi-racial society. What would Jesus' attitude have been in this situation? What difference would it make if Jesus' attitude were adopted universally?

5. Many people cry out for an end to war. Discuss whether there is a connection between our own private wars and the war in the world. What did Jesus say on this subject? What difference would it make if his teachings were widely applied?

6. Find out all you can about Jesus' attitude to money. When you have studied the references in the gospels, discuss what difference the application of his teaching would make to:
   (*a*) the ordinary person's attitude to his/her money and possessions;
   (*b*) the businessman's attitude to profit;
   (*c*) the attitude of everyone to taxation
   to the needs of others?

7. What difference would the wide application of Jesus' ideas about honesty make to such things as
   shops and stores
public transport?

8. Remind yourself of Jesus' attitude to love, sex and marriage. Discuss the effect on future family life and society which the universal adoption of his standards would make.

9. How does our inner attitude affect our actions? From all we read of Jesus, what do we see as the importance of prayer and worship to our motives and actions?

10. Read Paul's prayer in Ephesians 3 : 14–21 (*N.E.B.*).
    (*a*) What does Paul say God the Father can give us 'out of the treasures of his glory'?
    (*b*) What does Paul tell us Christ can do for us? (verse 17.)
    (*c*) In verses 18 and 19 what is he wanting from us (as he did for the people to whom he was writing?)
    (*d*) Which phrases in verses 20 and 21 tell us that where our powers fail and we only see a little of the way, God can take us much further?

11. With the last question and answers in mind, answer the following question:
    Which of the following shows faith
    (*a*) to aim at what we can do;
    (*b*) to aim at what needs to be done?
    Illustrate your answer with examples from Jesus' life and the lives of great people (such as those on p. 41).

12. What purposes do you think men and women of faith should adopt today in preparation for tomorrow's world?

Optional. Some of you may like to copy out Ephesians 3 : 14–21 as a suitable finale to this course of work.

BOOKS FOR FURTHER READING
AND REFERENCE

Andrew, Brother	*God's Smuggler*	Hodder & Stoughton
Augustine, Saint	*Confessions*	Penguin
Bader, Douglas	*Reach for the Sky*	Collins
Burgess, Alan	*The Small Woman*	Evans
Cartwright, F. F.	*Joseph Lister*	Weidenfeld & Nicolson
Collier, Richard	*The General Next to God*	Collins
Cousins, N.	*Dr. Schweitzer of Lambaréné*	A. & C. Black
Douglas, Lloyd	*The Robe*	Peter Davies
Fancourt, M. St. J.	*The People's Earl*	Longman
Fülop-Miller, René	*Saints that Moved the World*	Hutchinson
Gallico, Paul	*The Steadfast Man*	Michael Joseph
Garton, N.	*George Müller and his Orphans*	Longman
Hovelsen, Leif	*Out of the Evil Night*	Blandford (o/p)
Howard, Peter	*Frank Buchman's Secret*	Heinemann
Keller, Helen	*The Story of My Life*	Hodder & Stoughton
Kendall, J. & J.	*Man Alive*	Blandford
King, Martin Luther	*Chaos or Community*	Hodder & Stoughton (o/p)
Lean, G. D.	*Brave Men Choose*	Blandford
Morison, Frank	*Who Moved the Stone?*	Faber
Muggeridge, Malcolm	*Something Beautiful for God*	Collins
Prescott, D. M.	*The Senior Teacher's Assembly Book*	Blandford
	Readings for the Senior Assembly	Blandford
Roesler, J. H.	*God's Second Door*	Assn. of Mouth and Foot Painting Artists
Sayers, Dorothy	*Man Born to be King*	Gollancz
Schlink, Basilec	*Realities*	Oliphants
Scott-Moncrieff, M.	*Founders of Europe I and II*	Blandford
Sheppard-Jones, E.	*I Walk on Wheels*	Geoffrey Bles

| Thompson, P. | *The London Sparrow* | Word Books |
| Thornhill, Alan | *Mr. Wilberforce, M.P.* | Blandford |

Warner, Oliver	*William Wilberforce, M.P.*	Batsford
Whitney, Janet	*Elizabeth Fry*	Harrap
Wilkerson, David	**The Cross and the Switchblade*	Hodder & Stoughton
Wolrige-Gordon, Anne	**Peter Howard: Life and Letters*	Hodder & Stoughton
Woodham-Smith, Cecil	*Florence Nightingale*	Constable

*Paperback editions available

Reference Books

Allen Shaw, Wallace	*The Living Bible*	McDougall
Alexander, Charles	*The Church Year*	Oxford University Press
Cruden, A.	*Concordance*	Epworth
Harvey and Bather	*The British Constitution*	Macmillan
Platten, T. G.	*The Living Faith 1–5*	University of London Press
Wilson, Mary	*God's Hand in History*	Blandford
	1. *Pioneers*	
	2. *The Son of God*	
	3. *The Rushing Mighty Wind*	
	4. *Builders and Destroyers*	
Youngman, Bernard	*New Outlook Scripture 3*	Hamish Hamilton

Film

Mr. Brown Comes Down the Hill by Peter Howard
A modern story: If Jesus came today, how would he be received, what impact would he make, and what would he think of modern society?

Available as a complete film (approx. 1 hour, 20 mins.) from:

> Sound Services Ltd.,
> 269 Kingston Road,
> London, S.W.19

Also in four parts (approx. 25 mins.) with questions for discussion from: MRA Productions, 45 Hays Mews, London WIX 7RT; or apply to your local Education Authority Film Library. In Scotland application should be made to the Scottish Film Council Library, 16 Woodside Terrace, Glasgow C.3.